THE
THESIS
WRITING
SURVIVAL
GUIDE

"This is a masterful guide! Concise but rich in wisdom and practical advice, the authors offer step-by-step advice on how to make the process of writing an academic thesis more of an adventure of discovery, and less of an onerous task— and do so with elegance, clarity, and even a bit of humor."

Professor James J. Kennelly, Professor of International Business & Management, Skidmore College, New York (USA)

"This step-by-step guide is an essential tool for graduate and doctoral students. It covers everything from selecting the right topic to developing key writing skills necessary for producing a top-notch academic thesis. As a PhD student, I have found this book to be an excellent companion in own my thesis writing journey. It's definitely my survival guide!"

Michela Bearzi, PhD student at the University of Udine (Italy) and the University of Jönköping (Sweden)

"An engaging and very practical guide to the process of writing a thesis. It is full of practical, actionable tips which graduate students and doctoral candidates will find invaluable."

Dr Jonathan Stoddart, Lecturer (Teaching), Academic Writing Centre, UCL Institute of Education, University College London (UK)

"The Thesis Writing Survival Guide provides many helpful guidelines and tips to guide and motivate the student. The tone is accessible and engaging with a humorous undertone at times. Moreover, advice about the substance of thesis conceptualisation and writing is well-informed. I would definitely recommend this book to my postgraduate students."

Dr Arona Dison, Coordinator of the UWC Writing Centre, University of the Western Cape (South Africa)

"The perfect handbook to navigate the tumultuous process of writing a thesis. In this survival guide, the authors provide down to earth advice on how to avoid the pitfalls encountered by most students when writing their thesis."

Professor Olivier Furrer, Chair of Marketing, University of Fribourg (Switzerland)

THE
THESIS
WRITING
SURVIVAL
GUIDE

Research and Write an Academic
Thesis or Dissertation with Less Stress

DIETMAR STERNAD & HARRIET POWER

Concise books for smart learners

Our mission at econcise publishing
is to create concise, approachable and affordable
textbooks for a new generation of smart learners.

This publication is subject to copyright.

All rights are reserved, whether the whole or parts of the material are concerned. This is specifically applicable to the rights of distribution, reprinting, translation, broadcasting, re-use of illustrations, reproduction by photocopying machines or similar means (including electronic means), and storage in data banks and data processing systems.

The use of registered names or trademarks in this publication does not imply (even in the absence of a specific statement) that such names are exempt from the relevant protective laws and regulations and are therefore free for general use. Product liability: Despite a thorough editing process, the publisher can give no guarantee for all the information in this book. Liability of the author or the publisher shall be excluded.

econcise GmbH is not responsible for the content of third-party websites mentioned in this publication.

Paperback ISBN: 978-3-903386-16-7
ePub ISBN: 978-3-903386-17-4
Kindle ISBN: 978-3-903386-18-1

Copy editor: Catherine Tingle
Cover and chapter opening images: iStock.com/rasslava, iStock.com/koya79

First published 2023 by **econcise publishing**
© 2023 econcise GmbH
Am Sonnengrund 14
A-9062 Moosburg (Austria)

www.econcise.com

Contents

Introduction

There's just one reason why we wrote this book: **we want you to succeed in your thesis or dissertation project.**

If you're starting such a project, you've already come a long way in your studies—congratulations on all your achievements so far! Now it's time for the final adventure: writing your thesis or dissertation (we'll use the word "thesis" throughout this book to include both longer forms of academic writing). Admittedly, it's not the easiest part of your journey through the "academic jungle." You'll need to make important decisions along the way, such as which topic or research method to choose; complete an awful lot of tasks; and avoid pitfalls, from the lure of procrastination to accidentally plagiarizing other sources.

Finding your way through the undergrowth becomes a lot easier with the support of guides who know the terrain and can help you find the best path, circumvent the dangers, and provide you with tips and tricks that will enable you to reach your goal.

In this book, you are joined by a team of **two experienced guides** with complementary competencies. One of us (Dietmar) is a management professor who has successfully guided scores of graduate students from all over the world through their thesis projects for over a decade. The other member of your new support team (Harriet) is a professional editor who will share plenty of advice on how to actually write your thesis. Together, we have one mission: **to provide you with practical guidance that will help you successfully complete all stages of your thesis project.**

This is not a complete handbook of research methodology, though we hope you will find some useful tips for conducting your own research here. It is also not a substitute for the thesis and style guidelines of your institution (but be sure to familiarize yourself with them). We see our job as **supporting you with all the practical aspects of your thesis work**: how to plan your thesis project, how to approach and complete all the different tasks that are involved in it, how to write good text—in short, *how to really get things done.* That's why each chapter title also begins with the words *"How to …".*

Here's what you can find in the three parts of this book:

- **Part I** *Getting started with your thesis project* will introduce you to everything that you need to know for planning and managing your thesis. We will help you to get into the right thesis writing mindset, develop a project plan, find a suitable topic, become a smart reader of academic literature, and prepare a convincing thesis proposal.
- **Part II** *The main parts of your thesis* is a step-by-step guide through the process of completing all the main chapters of your thesis. We will share tips on how to find the right literature and write a good literature review, how to develop a conceptual framework, how to choose and correctly apply qualitative and quantitative research methods, and how to present and discuss your findings.
- **Part III** *Writing your thesis* provides highly effective medicine against the common disease of writing a thesis in incomprehensible "academic" language rather than in clear and concise English. Many students think that academic writing means writing in a very complex way with a lot of highly sophisticated words. Just the opposite is true: most advisors love it when students are able to present their arguments in a clear and engaging manner instead of in convoluted sentences (yes, advisors are human beings too—and, like you, they prefer to read texts they are able to understand). Part III will help you succeed in your writing. You will learn how to create a clear structure and flow to your text, overcome writer's block, cite the work of others correctly, and improve your own writing by looking at it through the eyes of a professional editor.

You can read each part (and indeed each chapter) separately, depending on where you are in your thesis project and on what type of support and advice you need.

The book is written with a focus on the typical needs of graduate and doctoral students in the social sciences. That said, we believe you will also find a lot of useful tips here if you are writing your thesis in another academic discipline or as part of your undergraduate studies.

Are you ready to get started? When you enter the jungle, it might still look quite dense and daunting. But with a little bit of trust in yourself—and with the help of the methods and tools from this book—you will soon get accustomed to the new environment and be able to chop your way through the undergrowth. The path is right there: you just need to take the right steps, one after another. It's a pleasure for us to accompany you, and we hope that this book will help you not only to survive but also to thrive on your personal thesis writing journey.

Access free bonus learning materials

Visit the book's companion website at *www.econcise.com/ThesisWriting* to get access to further resources for succeeding with your thesis or dissertation project:

- Printable PDF versions of two "summary sheets" (a **detailed thesis outline** and a **summary of a few key rules of APA style**) and an **Excel template to schedule your thesis project**.
- Useful **weblinks to additional resources** for each part of the book.
- If you are a lecturer who would like to use this book for teaching a research skills (or a similar) course, we can also provide you with **free, editable Microsoft PowerPoint slides** for your course. Just email *lecturerservice@econcise.com* to get them.
- If you want to stay informed about current developments in the field and get more information about new books for smart learners, **subscribe to our newsletter** at *www.econcise.com/newsletter*.

PART I

Getting started with your thesis project

Surviving your thesis project is so much easier if you are well prepared.

In this part, you will learn:

how to get into a thesis writing mindset,
how to manage your thesis project,
how to find the right topic for your thesis,
how to become a smart reader of academic literature,
and how to prepare a convincing thesis proposal.

How to get into a thesis writing mindset

Let's face it—writing a thesis can be an exciting task, but it can also be a big challenge. You could easily feel overwhelmed by everything you have to complete. You might face a lack of focus, concentration, and motivation. You might get frustrated when people don't want to participate in your research. Maybe there's a feeling of getting limited support from your advisor. And then there are the many hours that you need to spend working on your thesis, which could cause conflicts in your private and working life.

As with every big challenge, it will strongly depend on **your inner strength**—on developing the right mindset—to be able to successfully master thesis writing. "How you think determines how you act,"[1] says bestselling author David Schwartz. With the right way of thinking—with adopting a **positive thesis writing mindset**—you are laying the groundwork for success.

Know why

The first step for getting into a thesis writing mindset is to figure out the **purpose of completing your thesis**—to clearly understand the *why* behind your efforts.

So, why are you writing a thesis? Well, of course, there is the obvious reason: it is a required task in your studies. You just need to complete it to get your degree, which will then hopefully also help you reach your further career goals. So far, so good. If there's no other way around it, it's just a "must" that you need to achieve, whether you like it or not.

That's one way to think about it. A better way is to take a look at the additional—and more immediate—**benefits of writing a thesis**:

- You can become an expert in a field that you are interested in.
- It's a great opportunity to improve your planning, organization, and project and time management skills.
- You will create new knowledge that could help other people.

- You can improve your writing skills, as well as your critical-thinking and problem-solving skills (which are all in high demand from employers).
- It's a chance to connect with interesting people, such as your advisor, or the people you will interview during your research.
- You will learn how to stay committed even if things are getting a bit difficult, helping to improve your stamina, emotional resilience, and mental toughness.

The last point is particularly important. Being able to deal with unplanned difficulties and frustrations is a key competency for many jobs in our fast-changing world. You can see your thesis project as a great opportunity to learn how to deal with such situations.

What do you see as the most important benefits of your thesis project? Write them down. Make them explicit and visible (you could stick them next to your bathroom mirror). Frequently reminding yourself of the benefits of your efforts can help to keep up your motivation.

The power of attitude

"Attitude is everything," write Carol Roberts and Laura Hyatt in *The Dissertation Journey*. They recommend approaching a dissertation project "with a spirit of adventure, optimism, and a can-do attitude."[2] That's great advice to follow.

There's a big difference between:

- whether you see a rejected thesis proposal as a "failure" or a chance to develop a better version that will then be easier to implement;
- whether you get frustrated with not receiving any response from potential interview partners following your invitation email or take it as a hint that you need to change your message (learning what works well and what doesn't when you're trying to influence other people); and
- whether you see being stuck for what to write as an annoying writer's block or an opportunity for trying out a new method for getting your first few lines on paper.

Research has shown that more optimistic, "high hope" students tend to be more successful at problem solving and more resilient in stressful situations than their more pessimistic, "low hope" peers.[3] Especially when things are getting more difficult along the way, a **positive mental attitude** can make the decisive difference between success and despair.

Roberts and Hyatt suggest removing words like "can't" or "never" from your vocabulary (at least during your work on your thesis), and saying "Stop!" to yourself whenever you notice that you are getting into a spiral of negative thoughts.[4]

If you see obstacles as an opportunity to learn—if you replace *"This is too hard for me"* with *"I cannot do this yet, but when I immerse myself in the topic, I will be able to find a way to get it done"*—you will definitely raise your chances of making good progress in your thesis work (note the power of the little word *yet* here). As one of us (Dietmar) wrote in a book about the secrets of smart problem solvers, "with the right problem-solving mindset, every problem holds within it an opportunity to learn and grow."[5]

Tip!

It is easier to go through what can be a very lonely thesis writing project with a support team. Team up with one or more of your classmates, meet regularly, coach each other, and discuss how to deal with thesis-related challenges. You can also exchange parts of your thesis work and give each other feedback on it. Your personal thesis writing support team can provide you with valuable tips for advancing your research work, and it can also be invaluable for giving you emotional support during your thesis journey.

The prepared mind

"Failure in preparation leads to disaster on the battlefield"[6]—this is a quote from a strategy book of the US Marine Corps. What is true in a military context can also be applied to thesis writing. Spending some time and effort on planning and preparation can save you a lot of time (and headaches) during the writing process that comes later.

In a typical thesis project, there are **five major steps to complete**:

1. Choosing your topic and method (ideally chosen together)
2. Preparing a thesis proposal (including a preliminary literature review, which should be done as early as possible!)
3. Conducting a thorough literature review
4. Conducting your empirical research (data collection and analysis)
5. Writing your thesis

The important thing here is that each of these tasks builds on the previous ones. With a carefully chosen topic and method, you are laying the groundwork for a convincing thesis proposal. Your thesis proposal, in turn, will determine the focus of your literature review and empirical research. The results of your research will then form the basis of your final thesis. It works like a pyramid (see Figure 1.1): without having well-laid foundations, you run the risk that the bricks on the higher levels will collapse.

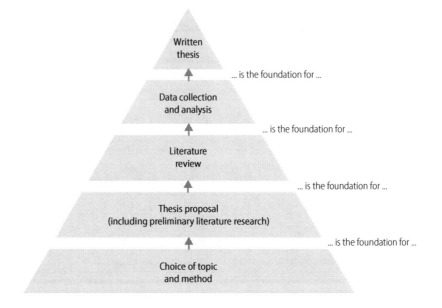

Figure 1.1 How one task builds on another in a thesis writing project

So, what does it mean for a thesis project to avoid "disaster on the battlefield"? The answer is simple, and you may have already guessed it: **put in enough effort to thoroughly complete the tasks lower down the pyramid!** Get these foundational tasks right, and you will be able to write a rock-solid thesis.

Good preparation can also make your life much easier during each phase of your thesis project. With a good **project plan and time schedule**, you will always know what you still need to do and how much time you have left for completing your tasks (see Chapter 2). If, before immersing yourself into the actual work, you have a clear plan of what you would like to achieve in a particular week or day, you will be able to focus on your priorities. Your later thesis writing tasks will also become much easier when, for example, you know your data analysis method before you start collecting your data (see Chapter 8), or when you prepare an outline before writing a chapter (see Chapter 12).

Time spent on planning and preparing will usually be a good investment. Be careful, however, that the preparation work doesn't become an excuse for not getting started with the "real" work.

The focused mind

Computer science professor and author Cal Newport conducted an interesting investigation into the habits of straight-A students. One of his most important findings was that the best students usually didn't spend long hours doing what he calls "pseudo-work" (such as staying up late without accomplishing much). Instead, he writes, "they gain efficiency by compressing work into focused bursts."[7]

A "focused burst" is an **intense work session in which you are able to fully concentrate on your thesis work without distraction**. That's not easy to achieve when the temptation of getting a quick dopamine shot by browsing through social networks, email or websites is no more than a click away.

But once you understand that these **uninterrupted blocks of "deep work,"**[8] whether they are 30 minutes or two hours long, are the key to productivity, you can use the following strategies to boost your concentration:[9]

1. **Schedule your deep work sessions.** Reserve time for "profound work" in your calendar, and protect it from other demands.
2. **Find a quiet place to work.** Whether it's in your own room or at the university library, go to a place where you are shielded from distraction.
3. **Eliminate technological distractions.** Put your mobile phone into silent mode (or even better, put it out of sight altogether), and close your email and social media apps. Get comfortable with not being available for at least a short period of time.
4. **Fight distracting thoughts.** If you notice that your mind is wandering to other topics, take a piece of paper, write the other thoughts down if they're important (to literally get them out of your head), and try to bring your attention back to the task.
5. **Work on one thing at a time.** Refrain from multitasking. There's plenty of research that proves it will just slow you down.[10] Give your brain a chance to focus.
6. **Take a break.** After a burst of intense work, give your body and mind some time to recharge. Eat and drink something, and take a short walk to get some fresh air.
7. **Make a habit of deep work.** If possible, get into a routine of scheduling your deep work sessions at the same time of the day or week. Use the power of habit. Once you are used to a certain working routine, it will get much easier to stick to it.
8. **Limit your deep work.** That might sound paradoxical, but setting a maximum time of deep work per day (rather than working "ridiculous hours"[11]) can help you to avoid draining your energy. You will be surprised by how much you can

achieve with three to four hours of focused work if you do that regularly, for example on five days a week.

Following these strategies will help you to become a thesis writing machine. After all, as Cal Newport summarizes in a simple formula: "work accomplished = time spent × intensity of focus."[12]

Fight procrastination

One of the biggest obstacles to completing your thesis is likely to be procrastination: delaying tasks until the last possible moment (or even beyond) despite knowing you might face negative consequences as a result. The word procrastination stems from the Latin *pro-* ("forward") and *crastinus* ("tomorrow"). So when you procrastinate you literally put something "forward to tomorrow."

We all know that this is not really a smart thing to do, as the work will then cumulate with tomorrow's work, the work of the day after, and so on—until we are unable to complete our tasks on time. But even if we know that, we are still often lured away from what we should be doing (working on our thesis) to whatever seems to be an easier way of spending our time (from watching Netflix to doing all those household chores we'd usually avoid). Thus, we might end up with a spotlessly clean room, but without a line written for our thesis.

If you want to survive, and thrive, in writing your thesis, you must fight procrastination. Here are a few expert tips on **how to get out of the procrastination spiral**:

1. **Use the two-minute rule to get started.** That's a trick proposed by James Clear in *Atomic Habits*, a bestseller about changing habits. The basic idea is simple: the most important weapon against procrastination is just to show up and get started. If you can "ritualize the beginning of a process," explains Clear, you are more likely to "slip into the state of deep focus that is required to do great things."[13] What you need, therefore, is a two-minute version of the task you are delaying. Instead of telling yourself *"I need to write a chapter today,"* you could just say, *"I will sit down and write one sentence."* This two-minute version of the task sounds much less daunting. Once you are actually sitting down and writing your first sentence, you have already successfully overcome the procrastination trap. Now the chances are high that you will add a second and a third sentence too.

2. **Use powerful self-talk.** "Screw it, let's do it" is the motto of one of the world's most prominent and productive entrepreneurs, Richard Branson.[14] It's the perfect anti-procrastination motto! The American author and philanthropist William Clement Stone recommended repeating the words "Do it now!" sev-

eral dozen times as a "self-starter" that will prime your unconscious mind to get started on your important task.[15] Whenever you think about postponing a thesis-related task, say "Do it now!" to yourself to fight the procrastination impulse.

3. **Record your excuses.** Cal Newport suggests writing down, "in ink, on paper," the reason why you are procrastinating as a way of showing yourself that most of your reasons are probably quite foolish.[16] It will enable you to quickly identify lame excuses like *"I need to hoover my room before I start writing"* or *"I'm waiting for inspiration"*—or prompt you to create an action plan to tackle more valid excuses like *"I don't know what to say"* (see Chapter 12 on how to overcome writer's block).

4. **"Make an event out of the worst task."**[17] That's another Cal Newport tip for getting particularly "horrible" tasks done. He suggests (a) scheduling that task in your calendar, (b) finding a new, special place to work on it (such as a nice café miles away from campus), and (c) telling as many other people as possible about what you're planning to achieve, so that it will be difficult for you to back out. As with all other strategies, the main trick here is to force you into getting started in the first place.

 **Tip!**

Here's a tip for advanced anti-procrastinators: use the "half-time system." Whenever you have a set deadline, try your best to complete the task within half of the scheduled time. For example, when you have two months left, try to get the task done within one month. If there are two days left, get it done by tomorrow. You'll have to complete the tasks anyway, and forcing yourself to do them sooner means you get them out of the way, you definitely won't miss a deadline, and you'll likely get through each task quicker too.

Celebrate small victories

There is hardly anything more motivating during a thesis project than making good progress. It's a great feeling when you've finally found your topic, when you're getting positive feedback from your advisor on your thesis proposal, or when you've successfully recorded the last interview for your empirical study.

A thesis project is about more than just getting the thesis itself written. In essence, it is a **learning and discovery process**—a process which you should strive to enjoy as much as you can. So don't just run from one task to another, but cherish all the insights that you will have, as well as all the small wins and big breakthroughs that you will make.

Take your time to **celebrate when you achieve an important milestone**—you can treat yourself by watching that movie you've long waited for, or spend a night out with friends, or just take another look at the piece of work you've completed and say to yourself: *"This is a really great achievement!"*

In the end, the main reward for your efforts will be the degree that you are studying for. But there are so many small rewards to be had during the process too—both intellectually and emotionally. It would be a pity not to consciously recognize and celebrate them.

 Thesis writing summary #1

- **Know the "why" behind your efforts.** Before you start working on your thesis, write down the main benefits you will get from it. Knowing your "why" will help you to keep up your motivation during the tougher parts of the process.
- **Don't underestimate the power of attitude.** An optimistic "can-do" attitude will help you to better navigate the obstacles and challenges that you will most certainly meet along the way.
- **Thorough preparation is the key to success.** Putting enough effort into the early stages of the process (choosing a topic and research method, writing your thesis proposal, conducting a literature review) will make your life a lot easier during the actual writing phase.
- **Work with focus.** Intense, focused bursts of work are usually more productive than working long hours filled with distractions.
- **Fight procrastination.** Ritualize the first few minutes of the writing process, use powerful self-talk ("Do it now!"), record your excuses if necessary, and make an event out of the most difficult tasks to overcome the tendency to procrastinate.
- **Celebrate your victories.** Take time to consciously enjoy your smaller and bigger accomplishments along the way.

How to manage your thesis project

A t first sight, writing a thesis the length of a short book can seem like a dauntingly big task. Like every big task, however, it will become more manageable once you break it down into a set of smaller tasks that you can then complete one after another.

In her wonderful book on writing, Ann Lamott tells the story of her 10-year-old brother who had three months to complete a big homework task—a report about birds. He had procrastinated until the last day (which, after reading Chapter 1 of this book, you would never do!), and was unable to start in the face of the huge pile of work that was lying ahead of him. That was when his father approached him, put one arm around his shoulder, and said, "Bird by bird, buddy. Just take it bird by bird."[1]

Bird by bird—let's take this as a motto for your thesis project too. After all, that's what it is: just a project consisting of a number of tasks that you need to complete one after another within a limited time frame. And as for every other project, you can use a few tried-and-tested **project management tools** to get it done.

Every good project manager would take at least three preparatory steps before starting with the actual project work:

1. Clearly **define the deliverables** of the project.
2. Identify all the **tasks that need to be completed to achieve the project objective** (in our case, getting your thesis written by a certain date).
3. Develop a **schedule** for completing the tasks.

Let's take a look at how you can implement these steps for your own thesis project.

What you need to deliver

Although the details can vary depending on the requirements of your subject and university, the **main deliverables** for a thesis project will usually include:

- a **thesis proposal** (a kind of structured outline or plan for your research project, also known as a "synopsis," based on a clearly formulated research question and the choice of an appropriate research method)
- a **literature review** (a structured summary of the relevant literature about your research topic)
- the **collection and analysis of empirical data**
- the **final written thesis.**

If you are studying in a graduate program, you might also have to give a **presentation** on your thesis before a committee (sometimes known as your "defense").

The single biggest deliverable during this project is your **final written thesis.** Let's take a closer look at what this typically includes.

A thesis (or a dissertation, or any research paper, regardless of its length) usually consists of the following **six parts:**

1. Introduction
2. Literature Review (Theoretical Background)
3. Method
4. Results
5. Discussion
6. Conclusion

These main parts of a thesis are complemented by **additional elements at the beginning** (such as the title page, sworn declaration, table of contents, etc.—collectively known as "front matter") and **at the end** (list of references and an appendix with additional materials—the "back matter").

Table 2.1 provides an overview of the contents that you will usually find in a thesis. The exact requirements can vary from university to university, so we recommend you check with your own department as to what's expected and amend this list accordingly.

Use Table 2.1 (or your own list) as a checklist when you are working on the individual parts of your thesis. This will help you to make sure you include all the important elements.

Part	What's included in this part
Front matter	• Title page • Abstract • Dedication page (optional) • Author's declaration (sworn declaration) • Table of contents • List of figures and tables • List of accompanying material • Acknowledgments (optional)
1 *Introduction*	• Description of the research problem • The research question and research aim (purpose statement) • Relevance of the research (including evidence from the literature) • Information on how the rest of the thesis is organized
2 *Literature Review* (Theoretical Background)	• A structured overview of the relevant literature • Theoretical framework (maybe also hypotheses if you intend to test theory)
3 *Method*	• The chosen research method (and why you chose it) • The sample (and the criteria for choosing the sample) • Data collection procedures • Data analysis methods • How scientific quality is ensured (objectivity, validity, reliability)
4 *Results*	• Reporting the results of your study in a structured way
5 *Discussion*	• Summary of the key findings of your research • Comparison of your research results with previous research • Contribution to generating new knowledge • Implications in practice • Limitations of your work • Suggestions for further research
6 *Conclusion*	• Answer to the research question • A strong "take-home message"
Back matter	• Reference list and/or bibliography • Appendices (including, for example, a questionnaire or interview guidelines, interview transcripts, detailed data analysis tables, or other relevant research material) • Glossary (optional) • Index (optional)

Table 2.1 Overview of the main parts of a thesis

From taking a first look at Table 2.1, you can see that there are lots of bits and pieces that you will have to work on. But don't worry: with good project management it will be much easier, as you can take it "bird by bird."

Get an overview of your tasks and timeline

Like any good project manager, the first thing you'll want to do is to break your thesis project down into manageable tasks. You can find an example of what project managers call a "work breakdown structure" in Figure 2.1.

Use this work breakdown structure or create your own that covers the main tasks you'll need to carry out to complete your thesis. This can help you to start planning when you'll get all these tasks done.

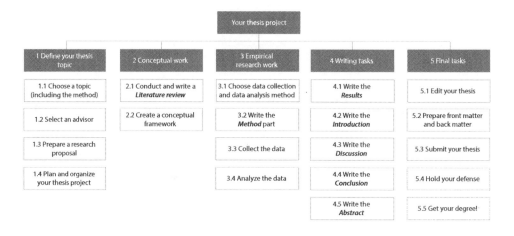

Figure 2.1 Example of a work breakdown structure for a thesis project

Once you know which tasks you have to complete, it's time to think about **scheduling**. There are three things to consider here:

- How much time do you think you need to complete each task (in hours/days)?
- When will you find the time to work on your thesis?
- What will the timeline for your thesis project look like?

The number of hours you need to get a particular task done will depend on your personal working style, but also on the targets that you set for yourself. You may have heard of Parkinson's law: "Work expands so as to fill the time available for its completion."[2] When you set yourself clear and realistic deadlines, you will improve your chances of getting your work done in time.

Take your work breakdown structure and consider each task separately. How long will it take to complete it? Figure out what each task involves. Other chapters in this book outline in more detail what's involved in each task. Choosing a topic, for example, involves doing a lot of reading, familiarizing yourself with research methods that could be a good fit for your topic, and talking to your advisor. Decide how many hours of work that might be, and realistically how many hours you can get done in a week.

When it comes to the writing tasks, work out a rough page count or word count for each section (your university may have some guidelines on this). You'll probably have a realistic idea of how much you can write per hour or day given all the essays you've written so far. Use that as a starting point.

Work out how many hours you can write a day, how many days you can work a week, and how many days/weeks it'll take to hit your word count. See Table 2.2 for an example of a **workload calculation** for the task of conducting and writing a literature review.

Basic data	
Hours available for the thesis project per day (5 days/week)	5 hours/day (25 hours/week)
Achievable writing pace (words per hour)	100 words/hour
Number of pages needed	12 pages
Average words per page	500 words/page
Total word count needed	6,000 words
Tasks to complete	**Required time**
• Literature research (40 sources x 0.5 hours) • Reading/processing the literature (40 sources x 1 hour) • Preparing an outline of the literature review • Writing the review (6,000 words/100 words per hour)	20 hours 40 hours 5 hours 60 hours
Total hours needed to complete the literature review	**125 hours**
Number of weeks to complete the literature review (total hours needed divided by hours available per week)	*125/25 = 5 weeks*

Table 2.2 An example of a workload calculation for conducting and writing a literature review

Use this information to create a **timeline** for your thesis project. See Figure 2.2 for an example of a timeline presented as a "Gantt chart," in this case created in a simple Excel file (you can download this as a template from this book's companion website, *www.econcise.com/ThesisWriting*).

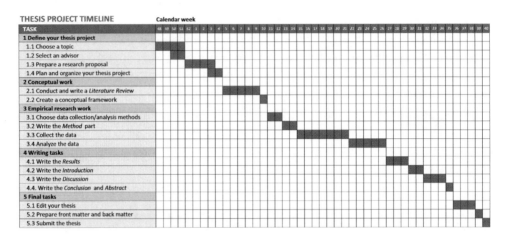

Figure 2.2 Example for a thesis project timeline

Organizing your time

You'll certainly have other important things to do in your life while you're completing your thesis. Maybe you have a part-time job, family or friends to take care of, or other obligations to fulfill. One of the most common mistakes students make is to give precedence to all these other obligations, and then never quite manage to find enough time to write their thesis (*"Maybe I'll find some time to continue writing my thesis next weekend"*). As a smart student you will face up to the truth: **you will probably never find enough time if you do not deliberately make time for your thesis.**[3]

Making time means actively scheduling your thesis work into your calendar, and then being committed to strictly protecting that time. If you really want to make sure that you will get your thesis project done within the limited time frame that you've got, consider the following three tips for **organizing your time** during your thesis project:

- **Make progress every day.** Mason Currey did some research into how some of the most productive creative people in the world organize their work. His findings are perfectly summarized in the title of his book *Daily Rituals*.[4] Many of the most productive people do not work long hours (although, admittedly, some do). Instead, they have *rituals* or *routines*, meaning that they use the same hours every day for their work. If you resume your work at the same time every day, rather than leaving gaps of days or longer between each work session, you will need less set-up time. Your mind will already be prepared from the previous day, and you can just continue the work without completely starting anew. What's more, you'll be motivated by that great feeling of constantly making progress. Don't wait for that one completely free weekend (the chances are high that it will never arrive): establish your own daily routine instead.

- **Work with, and not against, your biorhythm.** Schedule your thesis work for the time when you are most productive. If you're a morning person, work in the morning. If your energy levels are higher in the afternoon or evening, block out time for your work in the later hours of the day. Give your body enough exercise and sleep to replenish your batteries.

- **Schedule your work in uninterrupted longer blocks of time.** In his book *Two Awesome Hours*, Josh Davis uses research results from neuroscience and psychology to explain how you can "achieve fantastic levels of effectiveness"[5] when you focus your mental energy in a certain period of uninterrupted and undistracted work. Two hours is a good guideline here, as it is long enough to get a significant amount of work done (although the general principle also works with 60- or 90-minute blocks if you prefer to take more breaks in between). One of the most productive and successful authors in the world, Jeffrey Archer, also works in two-hour blocks, and he has a big hourglass on his desk to ensure that he will always work for the full two-hour period.[6] In Chapter 1, we noted that three to four hours is quite a decent daily dose of deep work. You could reach this goal with two 90- to 120-minute blocks a day.

During your work on your thesis project, you can also use the **"double to-do list"** method proposed by Oliver Burkeman for getting your smaller tasks done:

- Collect all the tasks you need to complete in the next phase of your thesis project on an **"open" list**. It can include "everything that's on your plate."[7] It can actually be quite long, but it will help you to get things out of your head and onto paper.

- That list will then feed your second, **"closed" to-do list**: a list with a small and fixed number of tasks, and ideally with only one priority task, that you can complete within a particular time frame such as one day. That will help you to focus on getting one thing done at a time.

In this way, "bird by bird," with one little task completed at a time, you will also be able to complete one chapter after another, and eventually your whole thesis.

Thesis writing summary #2

- **Divide your thesis project into smaller, manageable chunks.** Get an overview of all the deliverables and tasks that you need to complete before you start working on your thesis.
- **Use tried-and-tested project management tools.** A work breakdown structure can help you get an overview of the tasks that are involved in your thesis project. A visual timeline (or "Gantt chart") will tell you how much time to spend on individual tasks.
- **Don't wait until you *find* time—*make* time for your thesis work.** Deliberately schedule your work on your thesis project (ideally within a daily routine), and then stick to your plan.
- **Use the "double to-do list" method** and focus on one or a few tasks in one particular period of time (e.g. one day) to avoid being overwhelmed by the sheer number of tasks to complete.

How to find the right topic for your thesis

For many students, finding the topic for their thesis is one of the most difficult challenges in the whole research process.

Indeed, it's a really important decision to make. Your topic will determine what type of research you undertake, and the amount of time and effort that you will have to put into it. Your choice can also have a strong impact on whether or not you will be able to sustain your motivation.

What an ideal topic looks like

First, let's take a look at the basic criteria that your topic should meet.[1]

- **Choose a topic that you are excited and passionate about.** The more interested you are in the topic, the higher the chance that you will stay committed, even when things get a little more difficult along the way. Make sure that you choose a topic that will hold your interest for a long period of time.
- **Keep your topic specific and manageable in size.** A more specific topic (e.g. *"The effect of using a business simulation game on the learning motivation of undergraduate management students"*) is usually much easier to work on than a very broad topic (e.g. *"Innovative learning concepts and their impact on students"*). Many students fear that they won't be able to find enough literature if the topic is too narrowly focused. But it's usually the other way round—in most cases, it will be much easier to find adequate literature when you have a very precise research question to work on.
- **Make sure that you will be able to obtain the relevant data.** This is a really important point! Any topic that initially sounds highly attractive will lead to disaster if you aren't able to collect the data that you need to answer your research question. When you have an idea for a topic, therefore, think about which data you will need, and how you will collect it. Taking the example from above, there's probably a good chance that you'll be able to find professors who

use business simulation games and are willing to distribute a questionnaire to undergraduate management students. In that case, it would be quite easy for you to collect relevant data. It would likely be much more difficult, however, to conduct a survey among CEOs of Fortune 100 companies, as they probably wouldn't have the time or inclination to fill out student questionnaires.

- **Find a topic that is linked to relevant literature.** As you will need to ground your thesis in a thorough review of the literature, you can make your life much easier by choosing a topic that is well-linked to a particular stream of academic literature. Check out whether relevant literature exists before you commit to a topic.
- **Keep your advisor's interests in mind.** Your topic choice is always connected to a choosing an advisor. You will benefit from a supportive advisor, so check the interests of your potential advisor before choosing a topic, and try to get their support for your thesis idea.

When you are planning to conduct interviews, surveys, or questionnaires, keep in mind that only a small percentage of those who you contact may be willing to participate. The response rate is often not higher than 10 percent. It is therefore advisable to select a target group with enough potential interviewees. For example, if you need 10 interviews, try to find a target group in which you can contact at least 100 people.

You may also have to consider university- or program-specific guidelines when choosing your thesis topic. For example, does the topic need to be linked to a particular subject? Or do you need to make an **"original contribution"** with your topic? If this is the case, be reassured that "original contribution" does not mean that you need to make a groundbreaking discovery! It is usually enough for your research question to provide a new angle on a particular subject, apply a tried-and-tested method or theory in a new context, combine existing ideas in a new way, or analyze a dataset or case studies that haven't been analyzed in the same way before (see Table 3.1 for examples).

Original contribution	Example
An interesting thesis topic you came up with	*The effect of different leadership styles on the motivation of team members in Dutch advertising agencies*
Applying the method in a new context	*The effect of different leadership styles on the motivation of members of virtual teams in tech start-ups*
Applying the theory in a new context	*Can leadership styles theory be applied to teaching situations? Students' perceptions of the effectiveness of their lecturers' leadership styles in Scottish business schools*
Combining existing ideas in a new way	*Leadership styles and sustainability orientation: Do leaders with different leadership styles also differ in their attitudes toward their environmental and societal responsibilities?*
Analyze a new dataset	*The effect of different leadership styles on the motivation of team members: A case study in the French wine industry*

Table 3.1 Examples of different ways to make an "original contribution"

Some people also recommend choosing a thesis topic that will help you **boost your future career** by putting you in a better position to get a job in an area that is connected to your thesis topic. Of course, it would be great to find such a topic. But please do not put too much pressure on yourself here. Your future career is usually not dependent on your thesis alone. In the end, it is just one task to complete as part of your study program.

One of us (Dietmar) made a mindset shift from *"A thesis needs to be life-changing"* to *"This is a limited-time project in which I just need to prove that I can formulate and answer a research question in a structured way."* This was the key to transforming an almost abandoned doctoral dissertation that had not moved an inch forward for almost a decade into a manageable project that was completed within a few months.

The topic selection process

Now that you know the general requirements for a good thesis topic, how can you find your ideal topic?

First, be aware that the perfect topic will probably not just fall into your lap. Don't wait for that "great moment of inspiration"—chances are high that it will never come. It's usually much better to take a more structured approach to identifying your topic.

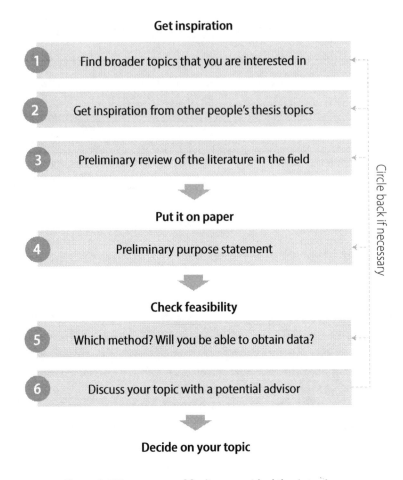

Figure 3.1 The process of finding your ideal thesis topic

Here's how you can go about it (see Figure 3.1 for a headline version):

1. **Find some broader topics that you are interested in.** Which courses and topics have you particularly enjoyed during your studies? In addition to your studies, you could also get some inspiration from your prior work experience, from academic or practitioner journals in the field, or from discussions with lecturers and your classmates. Make a list of several broader topics that you are generally interested in, and rank them on a scale of 1="rather boring" to 10="extremely interesting."

2. **Get some inspiration from other people's thesis topics.** Take a look at the theses that prior generations of students have written. Check out a dissertation database (e.g. the ProQuest Dissertation & Theses Global database if it's avail-

able via your university library—you can also ask your librarian to give you some tips on where to find theses and dissertations). This will give you some insights into what other people have already written about in the research areas on your shortlist. Use an online search engine with keywords like "educational psychology dissertation topics"—"dissertation" usually works better than "thesis" here—to get some inspiration from prior research in the field.

3. **Conduct a preliminary review of the academic literature in your field of interest.** This is *the* crucial step in the whole process, as you will need to find a topic that is related to and builds on existing literature. The more you read, the higher the chances are that you will find a really interesting topic that is also linked to an existing stream of literature. Visit your university library and search for journal articles in your field of interest. Check out Google Scholar and other databases of academic literature that are available through your university (e.g. JSTOR or EBSCO—see Chapter 6 for more information about how to find academic literature). Scan through the existing research in your field of interest, and find out what others propose for further research—you can often find such ideas for future research toward the end of the *Discussion* part of research papers. Literature review articles can be particularly useful to get an overview of the state-of-the-art research in a certain area (use, for example, keywords like "educational psychology, literature review" on Google Scholar). There are so many ideas that you can get from reading prior research papers in your field! Make sure to review a wide range of these papers before making the final decision on your topic.

4. **Prepare a preliminary purpose statement for your research.**[2] As soon as you have a few topic ideas that are linked to relevant literature, rank them again on a scale of 1 to 10 depending on your level of interest in the topic. Take your highest-ranked topics and try to formulate exactly what you would like to achieve with your research. For example:
   - "The purpose of this study is to *determine the relationship between* time spent on studying for exams and exam results."
   - "The purpose of this study is to *explore/assess/discover/describe/investigate the influence of/effects of/impact of* the use of technology in the classroom on student learning."

5. **Think about the research method that you could use, and check if you will be able to obtain relevant data.** Based on your purpose statement, which method would you like to use, and what sort of data will you need to collect? Do you prefer a quantitative method (e.g. a survey) or a qualitative method (e.g. case study research)? Can you find the data in secondary, published sources (e.g. publicly available statistical data) or do you already have an idea of how you

could collect data yourself (primary data)? Let us suppose that your research purpose is to determine the relationship between time spent on studying for exams and exam results. In this case you could, for example, conduct a survey among graduate students at your university. Will you be able to contact them via email with an invitation to take part in a survey? Ask yourself what sort of data you could use and do an initial check of whether you will be able to obtain it. Are there enough potential respondents, even if you factor in a low response rate to survey or interview requests? Checking whether it will be feasible to obtain relevant data upfront can save you a lot of headaches later on in the process.

6. **Discuss your topic ideas with your (potential) advisor.** Get in touch with a faculty member who you think could be a good match as an advisor for your topic. Present and discuss the purpose statement of your research with them. This statement will now be a refined version based on the method and data that you intend to use, e.g. *"The purpose of this study is to determine the relationship between the time that graduate students in educational psychology at University X spend on studying for exams and their exam results."* It's a good idea to have more than one topic ready for your discussion with a potential advisor, just in case they're not very interested in or are skeptical about the feasibility of your favorite topic.

You do not necessarily need to go through this process in a linear way. You might decide you need to circle back and consult the literature again after the discussion with your advisor (the importance of reading a lot of academic articles in the field before deciding on a topic cannot be overemphasized!), or you might want to revisit your data collection ideas based on the feedback that you receive.

 **Tip!**

Familiarize yourself with different quantitative and qualitative research methods before choosing your topic (see Chapter 8 for details). A good fit between the topic and research method is important for a successful thesis project.

When you have worked through the six steps above, you should have a clearly defined topic that matches both your own and your advisor's interests, which is linked to a relevant stream of literature, and that is manageable in size and feasible in terms of obtaining relevant data. That means you are ready for the next step in your thesis project—preparing your thesis proposal.

Thesis writing summary #3 ·······························

- **Start with your interests.** Which topics are you excited about? Compile a list of preliminary topic ideas. Rank them in order of your interest.
- **Read, read, read.** Reading (or at least scanning through) a lot of academic articles, as well as taking a look at theses and dissertations in your area of interest, is usually the best source of inspiration.
- **Before you fully commit to a topic, think about which research method and what data you will need for your study**, and whether you will be able to obtain the relevant data.
- **Prepare a clear research purpose statement** and discuss it with your potential advisor.
- **Keep it manageable in size!** Remember that the purpose of your thesis is not to change the world, but to show that you are able to complete a research project within a limited time frame and scope.

How to become a smart reader of academic literature

Finding, reading, and processing academic literature are key skills that you will need to master for all parts of your thesis project—from the very beginning, when you're trying to select an appropriate topic and write a convincing thesis proposal, to the end, when you will link your research findings back to existing literature in the *Discussion* and *Conclusion* parts of your thesis.

It can initially feel overwhelming to face the plethora of academic articles that have been published about a certain topic (it's not uncommon to have Google Scholar reporting "approximately 1.2 million results" for a particular keyword search). And when you've then found an article that looks promising, it can feel even more daunting to try to make sense of an incredibly dense text full of subject-specific jargon, citations, and technicalities about sophisticated research methods. It may seem almost impossible to understand for someone who isn't a long-standing expert in the field.

Don't get discouraged, however—we have some good news for you:

- There's **no need to read every article that is related to your topic**. You just need to find the most relevant sources—and there are a few search strategies that you can apply right away to quickly identify them.
- There's **no need to read academic articles in their entirety**. You just need to know how to quickly locate the essential information that you need—and below we'll share some tips about how you can do this without too much effort.
- You can increase your efficiency even more with a **smart note-taking approach**.

Let's take a closer look at how we can put all of this into practice, so you can find relevant literature for your thesis project, and read and take notes in a smart and time-efficient way.

What is academic literature?

You are generally expected to use **academic literature** as the basis for writing your thesis. That's basically all the "scholarly writing" about a certain subject.

Scholars (e.g. university professors or PhD students) share their theoretical thoughts and the results of their empirical research in academic (or scholarly) publications. The most common forms of academic publications that you will typically use and cite in a thesis are **peer-reviewed journal articles** and **scholarly books** (or book chapters). Conference papers and doctoral dissertations are further forms of academic literature. If they include important research results, however, these are usually also published later in peer-reviewed articles or books.

Textbooks (with titles such as *Fundamentals of Marketing* or *Introduction to Educational Studies*), encyclopedias, and other reference works are usually only "secondary" sources which summarize the findings from "primary" academic literature like journal articles and original research published in scholarly books. In some fields, citing textbooks or reference works in a thesis is therefore not seen as "academic" enough. Consult with your thesis advisor if you're not sure what is appropriate for your own thesis.

To help you distinguish academic from non-academic publications, here are some **characteristics of academic texts**:

- Academic publications are (usually) written by authors who are affiliated with an academic institution.
- Their target audience is other experts in the author's field, rather than the general public.
- They're written in a formal tone and contain subject-specific technical terms.
- They include citations and a list of references that can help the reader locate every source that the author used.
- They went through a quality check before being published, typically in the form of being reviewed and edited by other scholars in the field.

Figure 4.1 provides a **quick check of whether an article or book qualifies as academic literature**.

The reputation of an academic journal is usually measured by how often its articles have been cited by others. The commonly used *impact factor* measure, for example, reports on the average number of citations per article published in a certain journal within a certain time frame. You can find information about the impact factor and other journal ranking measures on the journal's website, the paid Web of Science database (you might be able to access this through your university library), or the freely available Scimago Journal Rank (www.scimagojr.com). Anne-Wil Harzing's Journal Quality List (https://harzing.com/resources/journal-quality-list), which is also free, is particularly useful for research in economics, business, and management-related subjects.

A publisher's reputation can also give some indication of the quality of its academic literature. A few "big names" in academic journal and book publishing include Cambridge University Press, Elsevier, MIT Press, Oxford University Press, SAGE, Springer, Taylor & Francis/Routledge, and Wiley-Blackwell.

Academic literature checklist

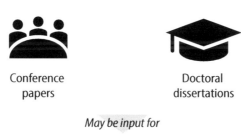

Conference papers

Doctoral dissertations

May be input for

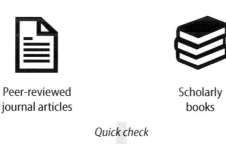

Peer-reviewed journal articles

Scholarly books

Quick check

✔ Authors affiliated with an academic institution?
✔ Includes citations and a list of references?
✔ Well-reputed academic journal or academic publisher?

Figure 4.1 Academic literature quick check

The number of times a piece of academic literature is cited is an important indicator of its relevance and influence within an academic field. The easiest way to check the number of citations is the "Cited by" function provided by Google Scholar. Be aware, however, that newer sources (published within the last couple of years) will only now be starting to gather citations. It is therefore possible that you will find some sparingly cited yet still highly relevant recently published articles, too.

In general, newspaper and magazine articles, social media and blog posts, reports from consultancy firms or market research agencies, and information-based websites such as Wikipedia and Statista do *not* count as academic literature. If you want to be on the safe side, don't use them for your thesis (although there are a few exceptions to this rule, such as when newspaper articles are used as data for analysis). Again, it's probably a good idea to consult your thesis advisor if you're not sure about a specific piece of literature.

How do you find relevant literature for your thesis project?

Google Scholar is a great starting point for your literature search. It's a blessing for researchers—a free web search engine that is focused on academic literature in all formats. For most academic articles that you'll find on Google Scholar, you'll at least get access to an abstract and citation details. For quite a few, you'll also be able to read the full text.

You'll probably also have access to other **academic research databases** through your university's library system. Some of the major databases of academic literature include ScienceDirect, JSTOR, Scopus, ProQuest, and SpringerLink, to name just a few. There are also specialized academic research databases for certain disciplines, such as EBSCO/Business Source Premier for business- and management-related research, and APA PsycArticles for literature in the field of psychology. ResearchGate is a social network for researchers that is also used as a repository for academic publications.

You should also be able to find scholarly books through your **university library database**. For many books there are also previews available via the Google Books search engine.

Whichever database you use as a starting point for your literature search, you'll typically work with carefully chosen **search terms** or phrases (including combinations with AND, OR, or NOT) to identify a list of potential sources for your thesis project (we'll take a look at more advanced search methods in Chapter 6).

Your search will then often result in a long list of results. You'll now need a smart approach to narrow down those results to a manageable number.

If you go through the results with the **"4R rule,"** you should quickly be able to filter out the most relevant sources for your thesis project:

- **Relevance:** from the title, and maybe from reading a few lines of the abstract, check how closely a source matches your research interests.
- **Recency:** can you find some recently published articles about your research subject? Most search engines and databases will allow you to limit your search to literature that was published within the last few years.
- **Reception:** how well-cited are the sources? Use the "Cited by" information in Google Scholar or in other databases to find particularly well-cited books or articles. Take a closer look at them, as they are likely to be the most influential contributions to the field.
- **Reputation:** take a quick look at whether the article comes from a well-reputed journal or academic publisher (see the tips above and below).

It might be helpful to compile a list of academic journals that are the most influential in your subject area. In most cases, there are no more than a dozen highly relevant journals in a particular research area. How can you identify them? You can ask your thesis advisor for tips, consult a subject-specific journal ranking, or take a look at which journals repeatedly appear in the lists of references in the relevant articles that you have already found for your topic.

You will typically find **three types of articles** in academic journals:

- **Empirical articles:** these report on research based on observations that have been analyzed with the help of qualitative or quantitative research methods.
- **Conceptual articles:** their purpose is to develop new frameworks, models, or theories based on the findings of prior research.
- **Review articles:** these summarize the current state of the literature in a particular research area.

Review articles can be particularly useful for getting a quick overview of the recent advances and "hottest" debates in your field of research. They often also include ideas for further research, which might give you inspiration for your own thesis topic. Try adding "review" as an extra keyword to your database search. If you can find a recent review article that is related to your research topic, that can save you a lot of work. It will usually provide you with a good overview of the prior research in a certain field.

Sometimes, you might also come across a **meta-analysis** in your field of research. That's a special type of review article that includes a statistical analysis of a range of prior studies on a certain phenomenon. It brings together prior research to identify overall trends in the data.

Use the 4R rule to identify a few articles that closely match your research interest. Three to five recent papers in the field are a good start. Then use smart reading techniques (see below) to get a first overview of the contents of these articles. If they seem to be particularly relevant for your thesis, you have a great starting point for **finding further related literature**, either by

- reading about interesting prior research in these articles and then locating the sources in the list of references,
- clicking on "Cited by" under the search result on Google Scholar to get a list of more recent literature that refers back to the article that you are currently viewing, or
- checking out the websites of top researchers that are frequently cited in the articles that you have found—you will often find information about their latest research there.

The more papers you read in a certain field, the more you will notice that there are some sources and authors that are referred to again and again. Make sure you take a closer look at those sources, as they are likely to be highly influential in this particular research area. Most advisors will want to see them being mentioned in your thesis too.

How to read academic literature without getting a headache

One of the keys to handling the large amount of literature that you will need to process for writing a good thesis is to learn **how to become a super-efficient reader.** There are two ways to achieve this: **reading faster** and **reading smarter.**

In Table 4.1, we have summarized some common tricks for reading faster. You can also search online for "speed reading" to get some additional tips.

What to avoid	What to do instead
Don't read the whole text from beginning to end.	**Get an overview of the structure of the text first.** Find out where the important parts are, and focus your reading on them.
Don't read every word in a text.	**Jump from one area of focus to another** and try to capture the essence of the meaning. Reading only the **first and last sentences of a paragraph or section** can also help you to get a first overview of the contents.
Don't subvocalize (speak the words silently in your head), as it will slow you down.	Though you probably won't be able to completely eliminate subvocalization, you can **use your finger or a pen to quickly move over the lines** (so you'll have less time to subvocalize). At the same time, you'll also reduce a phenomenon called "regression," where you unconsciously move back to words you have already read. Some experts also suggest **listening to music** (e.g. Baroque music) to distract your brain from subvocalizing. It depends on your personal preferences, however. For some people, it works well; for others, music can be too much of a distraction.

Table 4.1 A few strategies for reading faster

In addition to reading faster, and perhaps more importantly, learn how to **read smarter**. In essence, reading smarter means being highly selective in what to read and what not to read.

In most cases, there's **no need to read an academic article from the first to the last word** (and in between get a headache from the high density of information packed with technical jargon). Smart reading means quickly identifying and then only reading the parts that will give you information that is really relevant for your research purpose.

As a smart reader, you will always have a **clear purpose for your reading**. Would you like to get a quick overview of a certain topic or subtopic? Find a clear definition of a certain term? Or collect facts and evidence (or counter-evidence) for a certain proposition? Maybe you would like to better understand the research methods that other researchers are using?

Having a clear goal in mind before you start reading will help you to focus on what is really important, and spend much less time on reading irrelevant stuff (see Table 4.2 for an overview of how to approach the task of reading academic articles for different purposes).

Purpose of your reading	How to read in a smart way
Getting a **very quick overview** of the contents of an academic article	• Read the *Abstract*—it will provide you with a general idea of what the article is about • Read the first few paragraphs of the *Discussion* and *Conclusion*—you will often find a summary of key results there
Getting more information about the **current academic discussion** in a field	• Ideally, look for a recent review article in the field • In all academic articles (not just reviews), you will typically find a summary of the current academic discussion in the *Theoretical Background* section after the *Introduction* (which can also provide some further context)
Finding something specific, e.g. a **definition**	• Do a "Ctrl-F" search in a digital version of the article or book, e.g. with the keywords "define" or "definition," or use the term that you would like to find a definition for as a search term • Authors will usually define key terms when they are first mentioned in the paper
Understanding the **research method**	• Read the *Method* section to find out more about the chosen method, sample, and data collection and data analysis methods
Getting a more detailed overview of the **research results**	• Read the *Results* section of the paper • Take a look at the figures and tables
Understanding the **theoretical contributions** of a paper	• Read the *Discussion* in more detail—it will usually provide information about both the theoretical and the practical contributions of the research

Table 4.2 A few strategies for reading smarter

When you know what you would like to achieve with your reading, you can choose between one of the following **three basic modes of smart reading:**[1]

- **Scanning:** take a quick look over the material to find specific information or assess whether or not a particular source is relevant for your purpose. It's a precondition for effective scanning that you know what you are looking for.
- **Skimming:** look over the whole text quickly with the aim of getting a general understanding of what it is all about. You will not read every sentence here, but just pick out those parts that seem to be really important (e.g. headings, illustrations, or the first and last sentences of paragraphs in key parts of the paper).
- **Reading in detail:** this is when you're aiming to fully understand what the author is trying to say, for example by following all the details of an argument. Again, it's not about reading every single word. You will want to focus on specific passages that are highly relevant for you and then read (and maybe also

reread) them closely. A great way to read for detailed understanding is to process what you have read through note-taking (see below).

Smart reading means knowing the purpose of your reading, and then deliberately choosing the reading mode that is most suitable for that purpose.

As with all skills, the best way to become a smart reader of academic literature is to practice a lot. The more you read, the more proficient you will become in the different reading techniques.

Smart note-taking

Smart note-taking is about more than just quickly writing on a sticky note something that sounds interesting. It is a systematic way of compiling information that will help you to answer your research question.

Ideally, you will have a note-taking system that allows you to record your notes in a way that means they are **"ready-made" for use in your thesis**, so they are much more than just records about what you have read. These notes can include chunks of your own writing that can later be used in your thesis.

Here's how you can succeed at smart note-taking:[2]

- **Be selective.** Only record information that is relevant for answering your research question.
- Take your time to **record your notes accurately**, so that you can fully rely on them later without having to go back to the original source. Don't use abbreviations or other types of shortcuts. Being accurate from the beginning will save you a lot of time later during the actual thesis writing process.
- For each note that you are taking, record the **author or authors, publication year and page number of the source** (e.g. "Sternad & Power (2023), p. 23").
- Whenever you are taking a note, **put a full reference to the source into your list of references**. Some people use special referencing software like EndNote, RefWorks or Citavi, but you can also just simply copy and paste a reference into a separate Word file with the help of Google Scholar's "Cite" function.
- **Group notes about different topics on different pages** (or even in different files), and put them under headings that clearly describe the topic.
- **Beware of using material out of context.** A short quote from a text can completely misrepresent what an author intended to say. Adding a few additional notes about the context (e.g. the arguments that lead to a conclusion) can help to avoid such misrepresentation.
- **Make sure to always distinguish between three forms of notes:** (1) *direct quotations* (copying the exact text word for word), (2) summaries of what have you read in your own words (*paraphrasing*) and (3) your *own ideas and thoughts*.

The last point is of highest importance. Be sure to make a clear distinction between direct (word-for-word) quotations, paraphrasing, and your own thoughts when taking your notes. This will allow you to easily use your notes as a basis for your thesis text without falling into the risk of plagiarism (see Chapter 15 for more information about plagiarism). You can make this distinction, for example, by using different colors or fonts, and remember to always put direct quotes in quotation marks.

So how do you know which format to choose for your notes? **Exact quotations** could be needed as evidence for your arguments, when the wording used by the author is so perfectly "on point" that it's difficult to paraphrase, or when you would like to make sure that you are fairly representing an author whose views you plan to criticize.[3] In all other cases of taking notes about the ideas of others, it's usually better to use **paraphrasing**. This isn't just about changing a few words here or there. Correct paraphrasing means restating the text with different wording and a different structure while preserving the original meaning.

When you read and take notes, be aware of when the paper's authors are themselves paraphrasing. Don't make the mistake of representing these (paraphrased) ideas as the authors' original ideas. In such cases, you will have to go back to the original source and cite the original author or authors in your notes.

Figure 4.2 presents an example of smart note-taking. In these notes, all parts that are not within square brackets could be used directly in your thesis. Although you will most certainly not use in your final thesis all the notes you collect, with the help of smart note-taking you will already have gathered a lot of valuable "raw material" for your writing task.

NOTES ABOUT WHAT IS COACHING

Source: Sternad, D. (2021). Developing Coaching Skills.

[Note: include the following source in the list of references: Sternad, Dietmar (2021). Developing Coaching Skills: A Concise Introduction. Moosburg: econcise.]

[Definition of coaching] "Coaching is a purposeful interaction in which one person (the coach) uses a questioning approach to help another person (the coachee) think through challenging issues, raise their self-awareness, consider their options, and take the right actions to realize their full potential and reach their personal or professional goals." (Sternad, 2021, p. 6)

Most definitions of coaching fail to consider a team coaching setting where there is more than one coachee.

[Own idea, therefore in gray]

Coaching is not always conducted in a formal setting (Sternad, 2021, p. 8).

[That's a paraphrase of "Coaching does not necessarily need to be a formal process" (Sternad, 2021, p. 8)]

"Originally, professional coaching in an organizational context was often associated with getting people with a risk of derailing due to performance problems 'back on track.'" (Sternad, 2021, p. 16)

[The author then continues to explain how coaching has become a highly effective developmental activity for people without performance problems, too]

Figure 4.2 An example of smart note-taking

Thesis writing summary #4

- **Read with a purpose.** You won't have the time (or likely the motivation) to read every article word by word from the first sentence to the last. As a smart reader of academic literature, you will always have a clear purpose in mind about what information you would like to find, and will strategically select what and how you read with a clear focus on your purpose.

- **Identify academic literature.** If you are unsure about whether the source that you found qualifies as academic literature, answer these questions: are the authors affiliated with an academic institution? Does the source include citations and a list of references? Does it come from a well-reputed peer-reviewed journal and/or academic publisher?

- **Find relevant literature.** Start with a keyword search in academic research databases. Use the "4R rule" (relevance, recency, reception, reputation) for filtering out the most relevant sources, and use them as a starting point for locating further related literature.

- **Become a more efficient reader.** Read faster and smarter. Smart reading means knowing the purpose of your reading first, and then selecting an appropriate smart reading technique (scanning, skimming, or reading important passages in detail) for getting exactly the information that you want.

- **Use the power of smart note-taking.** Take notes in a way that means you can directly use them as chunks of text in your final thesis. Clearly distinguish between direct quotations, paraphrasing/summaries, and your own ideas and thoughts.

How to prepare a convincing thesis proposal

Before you start working on your thesis, most universities ask you to write a **thesis proposal**. This is sometimes called a **synopsis**, or a **thesis or dissertation prospectus** if it's shorter. It's a detailed summary of the research work that you intend to conduct. The purpose of the thesis proposal is not only to convince your advisor that you have thoroughly prepared and planned your thesis project. It will also help you to clarify exactly what you want to do, why you want to do it, and how you will do it, providing you with a map that will help you navigate all your future work on your thesis.

Advisors often find that the quality of the thesis proposal directly corresponds with the quality (and grade) of the final thesis. The efforts that you put in at this stage of the process are an investment that will definitely pay off later.

Although the requirements regarding the length and contents of the thesis proposal can vary (a typical length would be somewhere around 10 pages, but please check the specific guidelines of your university here), **a thesis proposal typically includes**:

- The title of your thesis
- Background information (research context)
- The purpose statement
- Research questions and the significance of your research

- An outline of the thesis and/or a preliminary table of contents
- The research method
- Your project plan/timeline
- List of references (bibliography)

Let's take a closer look at all of these elements.

The title of your thesis

The title should clearly reflect the contents of your thesis. It usually consists of two parts: a **main title**, a precise description of the topic; and a **subtitle**, which usually includes more information about the scope and method of the thesis. You don't need a subtitle if you can fit all of the important information into the main title.

A **good thesis title** will:

- Inform the reader about the subject, scope, and method of your thesis
- Contain the key concepts or variables that you intend to study
- Be concise and precise
- Reflect an academic tone of writing (not using jargon, slang, or overly catchy slogans)

Table 5.1 gives examples of good and improvable titles.

Title suggestion	Includes subject, scope, method	Contains key concepts/ variables	Concise and precise	Academic tone of writing
The Impact of Leadership Styles on the Perceived Stress Levels of Engineers: A Case Study of Three Teams in the British Semiconductor Industry	Yes	Yes	Yes	Yes
The Relationship Between Leadership Styles and Perceived Stress Levels of Engineers	Partly (method and scope are missing)	Yes	Yes	Yes
When Leaders Cause Stress: A Case Study of Three Teams in the British Semiconductor Industry	Partly: we do not know that it is a study among engineers	No: leadership style and perceived stress levels as the key variables are not mentioned	Not 100% precise	Yes: using a catchier main title is usually OK if it clearly conveys the main topic of the research (but consult your advisor first)

Title suggestion	Includes subject, scope, method	Contains key concepts/ variables	Concise and precise	Academic tone of writing
A Qualitative (Case-Based) Study of How Leaders and their Leadership Styles Can Have an Influence on the Perceived Stress Levels of Engineers Who Work in the British Semiconductor Industry	Yes	Yes	No: the title is too wordy; there's a more precise way of formulating it	Yes
Stress Test for Leaders: How to Ensure the Well-Being of Engineers in Your Team	No	No	No	No: that might be the title of a popular book, but is too informal for an academic thesis
When Leaders Cause Stress: A Case Study on the Impact of Leadership Styles on the Perceived Stress Levels of Engineers in the British Semiconductor Industry	Yes	Yes	Yes	Yes: using a catchier main title is usually OK if it clearly conveys the main topic of the research (but consult your advisor first)

Table 5.1 Examples of thesis titles

Before you submit your final title, show it to some classmates or friends. Ask them to tell you exactly what they think you will do in your thesis project after reading the title. That will give you some valuable feedback on whether the title is communicating the topic and focus well, or if you still need to refine it.

Background information and purpose statement

The first part of the thesis proposal (after the title) explains the **background of your study**. It will usually start with a brief summary of the relevant literature and prior research in the field, and will then lead to the **purpose statement**. Around 1,000–1,500 words will typically suffice for the background and purpose statement, but please consult your university's guidelines here, as the required length can vary from institution to institution.

The background section provides the context for your research. It briefly explains why the issue that you are investigating is important, and how it has been addressed and discussed by other researchers in the past. Keep in mind that the reason for including background information is to set the stage for explaining the purpose and significance of your own research. It is not a full-fledged literature review, so try to avoid lengthy treatises here and stick to the point. The logical flow of your argument is much more important than providing a comprehensive overview of everything that has been said and researched before on the topic.

Let's assume, for example, that your research topic is the impact of leadership styles on the perceived stress levels of engineers. You might want to address the following points in the background section of your thesis proposal:[1]

- **What is already known about the problem?** Here you might provide statistics about perceived stress levels of engineers, refer to literature on the negative impact of occupational stress, and summarize prior research results about the link between leadership behavior and stress levels in other professional domains.
- **What is not yet known about the problem?** You might describe a lack of research on what kind of leadership styles are causing stress for engineers.
- **Why is that important?** Because, you might argue, engineers are working on different kinds of problems and in different work settings than other professions for which the link between leadership behavior and perceived stress levels has already been observed, so they might perceive certain leadership styles differently in terms of causing stress.

After reading the background section, the reader should get an overview of what problem you are addressing, what others have already found out about the problem (don't forget to cite recognized authors in the field here), and what kind of further research is needed regarding the issue—a **"research gap"** that you intend to fill with your thesis.

The background section will then naturally lead to the purpose of your study. The **purpose statement** (sometimes also known as the **research aim**) clearly and succinctly summarizes what you would like to achieve with your research.

Here's one example:

> *"The purpose of this qualitative study is to explore the impact of different leadership styles of managers of engineering departments in the British semiconductor industry on the perceived stress levels of engineers in their teams."*

Does that purpose statement sound similar to the titles that we looked at above? That's exactly how it should be—after all, the title should reflect the purpose of your study.

Words that are often used in purpose statements are "explore," "develop," "discover," or "describe" for qualitative studies, and "determine," "investigate," or "compare" for quantitative studies.[2] Note that all of these words signify a spirit of inquiry rather than advocacy. It is not the purpose of a thesis to prove something, but to **find out more about how things are related to each other**.

Research questions (and why they are worth exploring)

The main purpose of research is to satisfy our curiosity about how things work in the world. The research question specifies exactly what you are curious about. It is the focal point of your research. For each part of your thesis, you should ask yourself "How can this help me to answer my research question?" (The assessor of your thesis will also ask the same question about your work.)

Once you have prepared a clear purpose statement, it is usually quite straightforward to transform it into a question. For the example above, the research question could be formulated as:

> *"What is the impact of different leadership styles of managers of engineering departments in the British semiconductor industry on the perceived stress levels of the engineers in their teams?"*

It is important for the research question to clearly define:

- which **main variables** (any characteristics that you can measure) you will investigate (in our case, this will be the leadership styles of managers of engineering departments, and perceived stress levels)
- what **relationship between these variables** you are interested in (in our case, this will be the impact of leadership styles on perceived stress levels)
- which **population** you will investigate this in (in our case, this will be managers of engineering departments in the British semiconductor industry and engineers in their teams).

The question *"How do leaders influence the stress of engineers?"* would not qualify as a precisely defined research question. It is formulated too broadly, as it remains unclear what the main measurable variables are—you cannot measure "leaders," but you can measure "leadership styles," and it is also much easier to measure "perceived stress levels," for which tried-and-tested measurement instruments exist, than merely "stress." "Engineers" is also an imprecise definition of the target population compared to "managers of engineering departments in the British semiconductor industry and engineers in their teams."

You can also break the research question down into several **subquestions**. These are narrower questions that specify what you need to know in order to be able answer your main research question. In our case, we could, for example, define the following subquestions:

1. How can we define occupational stress (stress in the workplace)?
2. How can perceived stress levels be measured?
3. What are specific factors related to the work of engineers that could have an impact on their perceived stress levels?
4. What do we know about the role of leadership behavior in influencing stress levels of employees?
5. Which different leadership styles exist?
6. How are different leadership styles linked with perceived stress levels of engineers?

When all the subquestions are answered, you will ideally also be able to answer your main research question.

In your thesis proposal, after clearly stating your research question and subquestions, you should add a few sentences about the **significance of your research**. The main question to answer here is "What will be the benefits of the results of my work?" You should ideally highlight the potential benefits for two groups:[3]

- **Benefits for practitioners:** how will your work help improve practice?
- **Benefits for academia:** how will answering your research question contribute to the literature (which knowledge "gap" will it help to fill)?

Here is an example of a very brief explanation of the significance of a study:

> *"A better understanding of how different leadership styles affect the perceived stress levels of engineers can help managers of engineering departments deliberately adjust their leadership behaviors in a way that alleviates stress for their team members. The research findings could also be used as an input for developing leadership training programs for companies that strive to create a healthier working environment, thus helping them to become more attractive employers for engineers in the semiconductor industry.*
>
> *This study will extend the existing research on the link between leadership styles and stress levels of employees in other domains (e.g. Abassi, 2018; Lyons & Schneider, 2009) by taking a closer look at the specific demands of the engineering profession in a fast-growing, high-tech industry."*

Outline and preliminary table of contents

A thesis proposal typically also includes an **outline of your thesis**—a short description of what you intend to do in the different parts of your thesis—and a preliminary table of contents.

The outline can be presented in a written form, providing information about what will be included in the different chapters of your thesis (e.g. *"The purpose of Chapter 2 is to review the literature on the link between leadership styles and occupational stress. This chapter will start with a definition of occupational stress and a short overview of the key factors that can influence the stress levels of employees …"*).

Alternatively, or in addition, you can include a **visual outline** which shows the "big picture" of your thesis. This is a graphical representation of the overall line of argument of your thesis, or the logical flow of your work. Take a look at the example in Figure 5.1.

As we can see in the example in Figure 5.1, the subquestions of your main research question can be good starting point for creating your own visual thesis outline. Answering the following questions can also help:

- Which subtopics will you need to include to be able to answer your main research question and subquestions?
- Can you categorize and cluster certain subtopics (e.g. everything that is connected to concept A—in our example, *perceived stress levels*—and everything that is connected to concept B—in our example, *leadership styles*)?
- How are the individual elements logically connected to each other? You will usually start with broader concepts and then narrow them down to get an answer for your specific research question. Using arrows you can also link topics that logically build on each other. One example from Figure 5.1 is that we need to know how to determine or measure both perceived stress levels and leadership styles before we are able to conduct the empirical research work.

Your (visual) outline can then be used to create a **preliminary table of contents**. Figure 5.2 provides an example.

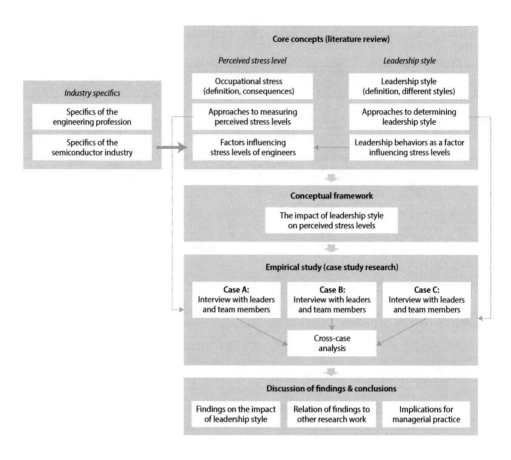

Figure 5.1 An example of a visual thesis outline

PRELIMINARY TABLE OF CONTENTS

1 Introduction
2 Theoretical background
    2.1 Occupational stress
        2.1.1 Definition of occupational stress
        2.1.2 The consequences of occupational stress
        2.1.3 Approaches to measuring perceived stress levels
    2.2 Leadership style
        2.2.1 Definition of leadership style
        2.2.2 Different leadership styles
        2.2.3 Approaches to determining or measuring leadership styles
    2.3 Profession and industry specifics
        2.3.1 Specifics of the engineering profession
        2.3.2 Specifics of the semiconductor industry
        2.3.3 Potential impact of industry specifics on the stress levels of engineers
    2.4 Prior research findings on the link between leadership behavior and employee stress levels
    2.5 Conceptual framework: The impact of leadership styles on the perceived stress levels of engineers
3 Method
    3.1 Rationale for choosing the method (multiple case study method)
    3.2 Sample
    3.3 Instrument design and data collection
    3.4 Data analysis procedures
4 Results
    4.1 Results of the individual case analysis
    4.2 Results of the cross-case analysis
5 Discussion of results
    5.1 Summary of key findings on the impact of leadership styles on perceived stress levels of engineers
    5.2 Relation of findings to other research work
    5.3 Limitations of the study
    5.4 Outlook: Possibilities for further research
    5.5 Implications for managerial practice
6 Conclusion

Figure 5.2 An example of a preliminary table of contents

As you can see from this example, the preliminary table of contents can quite easily be generated by combining the general six-part thesis structure (see Chapter 2) with your (visual) thesis outline.

Research method, project plan, and list of references

There are three more elements that you typically find in a thesis proposal:

- A description of the **research method** that you intend to use, including the general method, the sample, and the data collection and data analysis methods. (For more details, consult Chapter 8.)
- Your **project plan**—usually in the form of a timeline (see Chapter 2).
- A **list of references** for sources that you have used in your project proposal, and a **preliminary bibliography** of literature that you intend to use in your thesis. It's not your final bibliography yet, but it will show your advisor that you have already familiarized yourself with the relevant literature in the field (which you definitely should have done by this point in order to create a well-founded thesis proposal).

Once you've completed your thesis proposal, you have reached an important milestone in your thesis project. With a well-thought-through outline and project plan, you should now be ready to get started with the real thing.

Thesis writing summary #5

- A **well-crafted thesis proposal** is the best possible investment you can make for the success of your thesis project. Make sure to reserve enough time for this task—and get started with it as early as possible.
- A **good thesis title** informs the reader about the subject, scope, and method of your thesis, contains the key concepts or variables of your study, is concise and precise, and reflects an academic tone of writing.
- The first part of the thesis proposal contains **background information** about the research problem, its importance, and what we already know about it from prior literature. A **purpose statement** (or research aim) then succinctly summarizes what you would like to achieve with your own research.
- The **research question** clearly defines the main variables, the (suggested) relationship between these variables that you are interested in, and the population that you will examine. It can be further broken down into sub-questions. Your proposal should also be complemented by a statement about the significance of your research.
- A **written and/or visual outline and a preliminary table of contents** provide an overview of the logical structure of the argument in your thesis.
- The thesis proposal is completed with a description of your **research method**, a **timeline** of your thesis project, a **list of references** for the sources used in your thesis proposal, and a preliminary **bibliography** of sources you intend to use in your final thesis.

PART II

The main parts of your thesis

Surviving your thesis project is so much easier when you understand what you need to do in all the main parts of your thesis.

In this part, you will learn:

how to write the Introduction *and* Literature Review,
how to create a conceptual framework,
how to choose and describe your research method,
how to conduct qualitative research,
how to conduct quantitative research,
and how to present and discuss your findings.

How to write the *Introduction* and *Literature Review*

After working through Part I of this book, you should already have a good plan of action for your thesis project. Now it's time to get started with the actual writing task.

This chapter will give you some advice on how to write the first two chapters of your thesis: the *Introduction* and the *Literature Review*.

Writing the *Introduction*

The purpose of the *Introduction* is to introduce your research project to the reader. Although it comes at the start of your thesis, you'll probably find it easier to write the *Introduction* later on, after you've completed the *Literature Review*, and maybe even the *Method* and *Results* parts of your thesis. This is because it is only through reviewing the literature that you will gain a broader and deeper understanding of your research domain, the methods used in it, and the research gaps that still need to be addressed. This is all essential information that will help to shape your *Introduction*.

Even if you probably won't write this part of your thesis right away, let's take a quick look now at what is typically expected from the *Introduction*, so you know what you will need to work on:

1. **A few introductory paragraphs.** This "introduction to the *Introduction*" is usually untitled and includes a short overview of what your study is all about. The reader would also expect to find some brief information here about how your study will enhance theoretical knowledge and/or professional practice.
2. **Background to the study.** This is about providing some context for your research—about painting the big picture. "Some" context means that you

won't give a full-fledged literature review here, but you will include some reference to prior studies and how others have dealt with the issue that you plan to investigate. Thus, you show how your own work is embedded in a particular field of research. In this part, you describe what your area of study is, what other researchers have already found out about this issue (ideally with some contrasting views), and what remains unknown about it.

3. **The problem statement.** This is supposed to answer the "So what?" question after you have presented the big picture.[1] The problem statement explains why there is a need for your research. It could be, for example, an important issue that has not yet been sufficiently investigated in prior research, some controversial or contradictory findings that need to be resolved, or a societal or professional problem that needs to be addressed.

4. **The purpose statement.** You should have already formulated one (see Chapter 5).

5. **The research question.** This should also exist already (see Chapter 5 again).

6. **A short overview of the methodology.** This is a short summary of your method choice, your sample, and your data collection and data analysis procedures (see Chapter 8 for more details).

7. **The significance of your study.** This is about explaining the benefits of your work: both in terms of the theoretical contribution you are making—what does it help us to understand that we haven't understood before?—and in terms of how your research results will help improve professional practice.

8. **The structure of the rest of the thesis.** Briefly explain what the reader can expect from the remaining chapters of your thesis. You may also want to include your visual thesis outline here (see Chapter 5) to show how you will proceed with your research.

A good *Introduction* will be concise and to the point. In most cases, you do not need to go beyond three to five pages (although check your university's and your advisor's expectations here first).

Sometimes, the *Introduction* also includes **definitions of key terminology**.[2] In other theses, you will find these definitions at the beginning of the *Literature Review* (check your advisor's preferences here, too).

You might have noticed that there are some significant overlaps between what is required in an *Introduction* and the material that you have already prepared for your research proposal. That's good news for you—just use what you already have; there's no need to start from scratch!

Convention is to use past tense for reporting on prior research results, for example in the "Background to the study" section: *"Although Sternad et al. (2022) developed a theory on … there hasn't been any empirical work on that topic yet …"*. Then use future tense when you introduce what you're planning to do in the rest of your thesis: *"The data will then be analyzed with the help of …"*.

In Table 6.1, we've shared some ideas for how you could get started with the different parts of your *Introduction* (although you can of course start your paragraphs in completely different ways, too).

	Section of the *Introduction*	Ideas for how to begin the section
1	Introductory paragraph(s)	*"This thesis seeks to contribute to the literature on […] by exploring how […]"*
2	Background to the study	*"Research that investigates […] has become more frequent in recent years [include two to three recent sources here]. According to […], one of the main reasons for this growing interest in the topic is the increasing concern about […]. Previous studies in the field have observed that […] [include sources here]."*
3	The problem statement	*"The problem that is addressed with this study is […]. Several authors have noticed a potentially negative effect of […] on […]. This relationship has never been empirically tested, however, in the field of […]."*
4	The purpose statement	*"The purpose of this study is to examine the effect of […] on […] for [include the population here]."*
5	The research question	*"The main aim of this study is to answer the following research question: what is the impact of […] on […] in […]?"* *"There are several sub-questions that need to be addressed in order to be able to answer the main research question: 1. […]?, 2. […]?, and 3.[…]?*
6	A short overview of the methodology	*"A sample of […] will be used to statistically test the relationship between […] and […]."*
7	The significance of your study	*"Through investigating the link between […] and […], this study contributes to […]. A better understanding of […] will also enable […]. The resulting model can support […] in improving their practice in […]."*
8	The structure of the rest of your thesis	*"The remainder of this thesis will be organized as follows: Chapter 2 will provide an overview of […]. In Chapter 3, […]."*

Table 6.1 Ideas for how to start the different sections of the *Introduction*

What's expected in the *Literature Review*

In a typical thesis, the *Introduction* is followed by the *Literature Review* (this might also be called *Theoretical Background*). As mentioned before, however, we advise you work on the *Literature Review* before you start writing the *Introduction*. Experienced researchers believe that starting as early as possible with reading and analyzing the literature is "the greatest gift you can give yourself as a researcher."[3]

The *Literature Review* serves two purposes:

1. to **provide a structured overview of previous research in your field of study**, and
2. to **connect your own research to existing knowledge**.

Reviewing the literature will help you to gain a much better understanding of your field, and it will help the reader to better understand the context of your research.

A proper *Literature Review* is not a summary of everything that you have read or that has ever been published about a certain topic. You can—and should—be selective about what to include. Prioritize quality over quantity when it comes to your sources—aim to only include relevant ones. And don't forget to **contrast different views** and **take a critical stance** toward prior research.

Here's what is usually expected from a good review:[4]

- A **structured summary of the most relevant existing research** about your topic, including seminal contributions and the latest developments in the field.
- A **critical evaluation** of the existing research. You can, for example, discuss where there is consensus or controversy among researchers, highlight similarities and contradictions, or identify strengths, weaknesses, and gaps in the prior research.

"Structured" means that your review will include a number of subtopics, neatly arranged in subsections in which you group information about similar studies into coherent topics or themes. You can then compare and contrast the studies within each subsection and draw your conclusions from this.[5]

There are **four steps for conducting your review**:

1. Identify relevant literature.
2. Read and critically analyze the literature.
3. Organize the literature (identify the main themes and decide on a structure for your review).
4. Write the *Literature Review*, with an introduction, main body (based on your chosen organizational structure), and conclusion.

The *Literature Review* or *Theoretical Background* chapter of a thesis sometimes also includes the development of a **conceptual model** or of **hypotheses** based on the review of prior literature. We will focus on that aspect in more detail in Chapter 7. First, let's take a closer look at each of the four steps above.

Identify relevant literature

Your first task is to **identify literature that is relevant for answering your research question**. In Chapter 4, we discussed how you can distinguish academic literature from non-academic sources, and how you can use academic databases to locate journal articles (the premier source of up-to-date research) and your online library catalogue to find relevant scholarly books.

As there's a plethora of academic literature out there, you will need a **smart search strategy** to find those sources that are particularly relevant for your research project.

You could, for example, get started with jotting down a few first thoughts about concepts and subtopics that are related to your research question. A **concept map** (see Figure 6.1 on page 67), in which you use lines and arrows to represent how key concepts and ideas are related to each other, is a very useful tool for that purpose.

You can derive **relevant keywords** from the title of your thesis, as well as from the research question and sub-questions that you have formulated in your thesis proposal (see Chapter 5). The more precisely you formulated your research questions in the first place, the easier it will be for you to get started with a focused keyword search.

Let's take the example of the research question that we formulated in the previous chapter:*"What is the impact of different leadership styles of managers of engineering departments in the British semiconductor industry on the perceived stress levels of the engineers in their teams?"*

There are two main concepts (or variables) here—leadership styles and perceived stress levels—and there is a population that the research is focused on: managers and team members in engineering departments in the British semiconductor industry.

You can use **Boolean operators** (words or symbols that combine or exclude keywords) in your search. Different databases use different Boolean operators, so you might first want to check the conventions for the database you are intending to use.

Here are a few examples of Boolean operators that you could use in a search on **Google Scholar** (quotation marks mean that you are searching for an exact phrase):

- **AND** will only lead to results in which all search terms are included, for example *"leadership styles" AND "stress levels"* (with the aim of identifying research about the links between those two variables), or *stress AND engineers AND British* (to identify research about stress in the target population).

- **OR** will lead to results that include either search term, for example *engineers AND ("work stress" OR "occupational stress" OR "professional stress")* for getting results that include both the keyword "engineers" and at least one of the three keywords that are linked with an OR in parentheses (round brackets). Note that you can use parentheses to group elements that should be searched for together first before relating them to the other terms—just as in a math equation.
- **- (hyphen)** to exclude a certain term from the search, for example *engineer AND stress -plant* (to exclude articles that are related to stress levels of engineered plants).
- **AROUND** to locate terms that appear close to each other in the text, for example *"stress levels" AROUND (3) engineers* (for identifying research results in which the terms "stress levels" and "engineers" appear within three words of each other).

Some databases will also allow you to work with **wildcards**, such as a question mark (?) for replacing one character, for example *wom?n* to find both *woman* and *women*, or an asterisk (*) for including different endings, such as *enginee** for *engineer*, *engineers*, and *engineering*.

Most databases will also allow you to conduct an **advanced search**, in which you can, for example, limit your search to certain authors, journals, or periods of publication.

Make sure to include synonyms or similar terms in your search, such as both *"work stress"* and *"occupational stress."* You can also try to use opposites, such as *"well-being"* instead of *"work stress."*

 **Tip!**

Try to find review articles or meta-analyses about your topic—studies that use statistical methods to identify trends by combining data from several prior studies on the same subject. Use, for example, *"keyword A" AND review* or *"keyword A" AND meta-analysis* for your search. These two types of articles can provide you with a quick and comprehensive overview of prior research in the field.

The most important thing that you should keep in mind when you conduct your search is that the literature should always be **related to your research problem and research question**. It is not your task to write a textbook about the fundamentals of your discipline, but to provide relevant context for your own research.

Once you have found highly relevant articles, you can also use the **list of references** at the end of these articles, or the **"Cited by"** function in Google Scholar or other databases, to identify closely related research papers.

Although you will certainly want to include some sources that strongly influenced the development of your field of research in the past, try to put the emphasis on more recent research.

Try to be systematic. Document which databases you search, which period of time you cover, and which keywords you use. Set clear criteria for including or excluding articles from the search results (e.g. "I'll only consider studies about the link between leadership behaviors and stress levels" or "I'll exclude articles that report on non-work-related stressors"). You could also classify the sources you find into *seminal sources* (cited in almost all the research papers in the field), *priority A sources* (highly relevant for your study), and *priority B sources* (other interesting sources that are not closely linked to your research question). It is good practice to record the steps that you have been taking to develop your *Literature Review*, and this includes your search of the literature.

Read and critically analyze the literature

As soon as you have found a few promising sources, start reading them. Every article will help you better understand the discussions that are going on in your field, and can also give you new ideas for organizing your review. Be smart in **choosing the right reading techniques** (see Chapter 4): instead of reading every article from the first word to the last, use scanning and skimming for "priority B" literature (see the tip above), and selected in-depth reading for seminal and "priority A" literature.

Use **smart note-taking** (also discussed in Chapter 4) to summarize key points from each article or book. Make sure to maintain an ongoing accurate bibliography, so that you don't have to research the references twice.

When you write a thesis, it's important to **read critically**:

- Don't take for granted that everything you read is necessarily "true."
- Ask yourself questions about what you are reading. For example: "Are the findings of the study context-specific?", "What are the strengths and weaknesses of this research?", "What assumptions are made by the authors—and are these assumptions reasonable?", "Which data and methods were used?", and "What's missing in the discussion?"
- Focus on the arguments that are presented. Are they logical, fact-based, and relevant? Are there counter-arguments or conflicting evidence?

Don't forget to note down your **critical thoughts** as you write your notes. This will also be a good preparation for **critical writing**, which you need for building up a convincing argument in your thesis. We will discuss critical writing later, on page 172 in Chapter 14.

One very effective way of analyzing the literature is a **literature review matrix**. This is a table in which you collect details in a structured way about all the relevant sources connected to a particular subtopic or theme. Note that you will usually have one summary table per theme or sub-question, not one table for everything.

Table 6.2 shows a simple example of a literature review matrix—in this case focused on collecting research results and arguments about the link between leadership behavior and stress levels of employees. Once you have summarized in such a matrix one or two dozen articles that are related to one theme, you will begin to see patterns in the results and arguments that will enable you to write a coherent summary of the research findings in that particular domain.

Of course, it is also possible to extend your matrix with additional columns (e.g. implications for practice, limitations, or your own comments). If you type in "example literature matrix" in a search engine, you can get further inspiration about different approaches to structuring such a summary table.

Source	Theoretical basis / conceptual framework	Method	Key results / main arguments regarding the relationship between leadership behavior and experienced stress levels of employees
Offermann & Hellmann (1996)	Leader support as a moderator of employee stress levels	Quantitative study among 343 mid-level managers of a multinational bank	Leader behaviors can have a significant influence on the experienced stress levels of employees. There are leader behaviors for which both leaders and employees see a link to stress levels (e.g. applying pressure), and others where only employees see the association with stress levels (e.g. limited participation).
Newton et al. (2020)	Conservation of Resources Theory and the Job Demand Resources Model	Quantitative study among 518 employees of a large government department	The vision of leaders (on different organizational levels) can have an impact on how employees can adjust to different work stressors. It is not only the behavior of the immediate managers that can have an impact on perceived stress levels of employees, but also the vision of higher-level leaders.
…	…	…	…

Table 6.2 An example of a literature review matrix

Organize the literature

There's one thing that you should definitely avoid in your *Literature Review*, and that's what Roberts and Hyatt call "disorganized ramblings."[6] Your review should have a clear structure that organizes the literature into topics that are related to each other, and it should **follow a logical framework**.

You could structure your review (or parts of it) in any of the following ways.

- **Sequentially** (or chronologically)—especially when you would like to describe how the discussion about a topic or area of research has evolved over time. This does not mean that you need to order your sources precisely by publication date, but that you should more generally describe how thematical trends progressed over time.
- **Thematically**—where you break down a topic into several subtopics, issues, or themes, which you then review and discuss one after another.

- **From broad to specific**—where you start with the more general context, and then progressively narrow down to the issues that are more closely connected with your specific research question (this is also called the "funnel" approach).[7]

You can use the literature review matrix (see Table 6.2) as a tool to organize the literature you've found. It will help you to identify patterns and themes, and commonalities and differences in prior research. Alternatively, you can use a **synthesis matrix**, which allows you to categorize the different ideas, arguments, or themes that you find in different sources (see Table 6.3 for an example).

Significant ideas / common themes / main arguments	Stewart (2022)	Frank et al. (2020)	Myers & Brinkman (2017)	Galiano (2021)
Leader support leads to lower perceived stress levels	If leaders and followers have different perceptions of leader support, followers tend to experience higher stress levels (p. 233)	The link between leader support and lower perceived stress levels is higher for younger than older employees (p. 322)	-	A strong relationship between leader support and lower stress levels of employees was observed in a government agency (pp. 435–436)
Exerting pressure leads to higher perceived stress levels	-	"Younger employees are more immune to pressure exerted by their leaders than older employees" (p. 327)	Perceived pressure has a stronger negative impact on employee stress levels in Asia than in the US (p. 45)	Pressure was only a minor factor that contributed to the perceived stress levels of employees in a government agency (p. 432)
…	…	…	…	…

Table 6.3 A simplified example of a synthesis matrix

In a synthesis matrix (like the one in Table 6.3), list in the first column some key arguments or ideas that you've found in the literature. As you read and work through more articles, you can add either direct quotations or your own brief summaries in the following columns. In this way, you'll start to recognize patterns, overlaps, contradicting evidence, and gaps. This can form a good basis for synthesizing the literature in a coherent way.

You could also use a **concept map** to organize the subtopics that you have found in the literature, and then create an outline from it (see Figure 6.1 for an example which uses a different research topic from the one we've been focusing on).

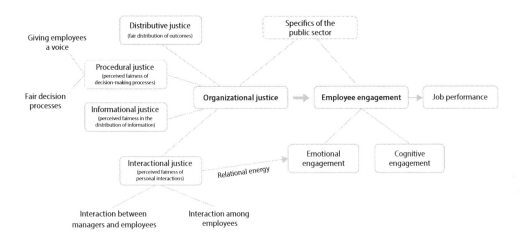

Figure 6.1 A concept map for the research question "What is the effect of perceived organizational justice on employee engagement in the public sector?"

A corresponding outline of subsections for the *Literature Review* based on the concept map in Figure 6.1 could look like this:

Organizational Justice
    Distributive Justice
    Procedural Justice
        Fair Decision Processes
        Giving Employees a Voice
    Informational Justice
    Interactional Justice
        Interaction Between Managers and Employees
        Interaction Among Employees

Employee Engagement
    Emotional Engagement
    Cognitive Engagement
    Employee Engagement and Job Performance

The Link Between Organizational Justice and Employee Engagement
    Distributive Justice and Employee Engagement
    Procedural Justice and Employee Engagement
    Informational Justice and Employee Engagement
    Interactional Justice and Employee Engagement
    Relational Energy as a Key Factor of Determining Employee Engagement

Employee Engagement in the Public Sector
    Specifics of Organizational Justice in the Public Sector
        Distributive Justice in the Public Sector
        Procedural Justice in the Public Sector
        Informational Justice in the Public Sector
        Interactional Justice in the Public Sector
    Specifics of Employee Engagement in the Public Sector

A Conceptual Model of the Link Between Organizational Justice and Employee Engagement in the Public Sector

As you can see, this outline combines a thematical structure (breaking down the topic into subtopics) with a "funnel" approach, in which the broader concepts of organizational justice and employee engagement are explored first before narrowing down to the specifics of how these two concepts are related to each other in the public sector.

Write the *Literature Review*

Once you have found, analyzed, and organized the relevant literature, it's time to get started with the actual writing task.

The *Literature Review* will usually begin with an **introduction** in which you briefly describe the aim and scope of the review, the approach that you used to identify relevant literature, and the structure of your review.

The **main body** of the *Literature Review* presents different subtopics structured in a logical way. You can provide a bit of background information to explain the context of your research here, but the majority of your review should be focused on the variables that you aim to investigate with your research question.

Each subsection in the main body will start with one or two **introductory sentences** in which you explain what it's about (e.g. *"This section presents three different models of cultural dimensions"*). This is followed by a **presentation of the findings from previous research** (including arguments, counter-arguments, and related evidence). Finally, you should include a short **summary and conclusion** that links the findings from that particular subsection back to the focus of interest of your own study.

One of the most common mistakes that students make is to just write the review as a string of disjointed (and rather dull) summaries of what other authors have said about a topic (*"Jones observed …"*, *"Peterson said …"*, *"Chang found …"*). The aim of the *Literature Review* is not to present all that has ever been said about a topic or to collect the best quotations from the work of other writers. It is better to think about the *Literature Review* as a **coherent story** in which you explain to someone who does not know much about your topic what is already known, what is contested, and what remains to be explored in your particular field of research—and to tell this story in an interesting and engaging way.

A good *Literature Review* is much more than a summary of the literature. You should also try to **synthesize the literature**. This means you should:[8]

- make **connections** between different studies (e.g. which studies were based on others)
- highlight **commonalities and similarities** as well as **differences, contradictions, and inconsistencies** between theories and empirical research findings
- discuss issues with **arguments both for and against them**
- explain **how ideas have evolved or changed over time**
- identify **gaps in the literature**.

Remember to take a critical approach to the literature, and do not forget to discuss conflicting views and perspectives.

After you have compared different research results, include a **summary and conclusion** not only at the end of each subsection as we have discussed above, but also at the end of each major section. Link the essence of prior research findings back to your own research question. After all, that's what the review is all about—providing context for and informing your own research.

The *Literature Review* often (but not always) culminates in the **development of a conceptual model** and/or **deriving hypotheses** that you will then test in an empirical study. We will explain in more detail how you can go about these theory building tasks in the next chapter.

Thesis writing summary #6

- **Write the *Introduction* later in your research project.** The *Introduction* provides a concise overview of the context and background, purpose, research question, methodology, and significance of your research. Many (if not all) of these points will become more clearly defined based on the information that you will gather during your *Literature Review*.

- **Follow four essential steps to conduct your *Literature Review*.** 1. identify relevant literature (the word "relevant" is important here), 2. read and critically analyze the literature, 3. organize the literature in a structured way, and 4. write your review with an introduction, main body (following your chosen organizational framework), and conclusion.

- **Use a smart search strategy to identify relevant literature.** Select keywords based on your research question, use Boolean operators to narrow down your search, and prioritize the search results. Then read selectively and critically, and take smart notes that you will then be able to use in your thesis.

- **Organize the literature.** Tools like a literature review matrix or a synthesis matrix can help you identify patterns, themes, or potential contradictions in the literature. Use a logical organizational framework (e.g. sequential, thematical, or from broad to specific), concept maps, and outlines to break down your review into subtopics before you start writing.

- **Write your *Literature Review* in a structured way.** Use an *introduction–main body–conclusion* structure both for the review as a whole and for each subsection. Make sure to not only summarize but synthesize the literature, juxtaposing, discussing, and integrating different arguments and research results.

How to create a conceptual framework

After you've completed the main parts of your *Literature Review*, it's time to condense the essence of your findings into a **conceptual framework** (which is often also called a **theoretical framework**, especially if it is derived from published theories).[1] Merriam and Tisdell, in their book on qualitative research, wrote that a colleague of theirs once remarked "that if she could have figured out what a theoretical framework was early on, she could have cut a year off of her graduate studies!"[2]

In this chapter, we will unveil the mysteries of this secret "shortcut." We'll start with a quick overview of what a conceptual framework is and why you need one. Then we'll provide you with some practical tips on how to develop your own conceptual framework for your thesis.

What is a conceptual framework and why do we need it?

A conceptual framework is a written or visual **representation of the expected relationship(s) between the main variables you are studying** (remember that variables are any factors or characteristics that you can measure).

In many cases, you will find the conceptual framework at the end of the *Literature Review* in a thesis. It's actually a **lynchpin between what you have found in the literature and your own empirical work**, in which you will usually test whether the relationships between variables that you have proposed in your conceptual framework really exist.

Be aware, however, that there are also certain approaches to empirical research in which you do not work with a preconceived conceptual framework. Grounded theory, as one approach to qualitative research, is a salient example here (see Chapter 9). Theoretical deliberations do not derive from the literature in this case, but emerge from the data. This does not mean that you can't have a conceptual framework—it is just developed later in the process, and the source is a different one (your own data instead of the literature or published theories). In such a case, you will present your conceptual framework in the *Discussion* part of the thesis rather than at the end of your *Literature Review*. But it will still be there.

In any event, creating a conceptual framework is a key step in building a **theory: a concise and well-founded (yet tentative) explanation of certain phenomena that we can repeatedly observe in the real world**.

You can consider a theory as a bit more than a conceptual framework. It also includes a crystal-clear definition of concepts and variables, and explains—with compelling arguments, usually based on existing knowledge and theories, and ideally as simply and yet as precisely as possible—how the variables are related to each other.

Some students see a difference between how things work "in theory" (i.e. in books and research articles) and "in practice" (i.e. in the "real world"), and then typically "prefer" practice over theory. That's a common misperception based on using the word "theory" in an everyday sense (where "works in theory" is sometimes equated with "does not work in practice").

Actually, theory and practice are not two antagonistic concepts. Theories are vital for enabling us to understand how the world works. They help us make predictions and figure out what we can do to change things for the better. Theories enable us to reflect on what we do in practice, and our theories about how things work fundamentally shape our practical behavior.

Developing theories that help us understand and influence certain phenomena in our world is a core purpose of research. A solid conceptual framework is an important milestone on the way to creating a useful theory. For the purpose of writing a compelling thesis, the conceptual framework is a key tool for clearly and unambiguously illustrating what the main concepts of your research are and how they are related to each other.

With a clear conceptual framework in place based on your literature review, you will know exactly what to look for in your empirical work, as you can focus your research on the concepts that are part of your framework. It will also make your life easier when you later try to link the results of your empirical work back to prior research results and existing theories in the *Discussion* part of your thesis (see Chapter 11).

How to come up with a conceptual framework

OK, enough of all that theory about theories. Let's get practical. Here are three concrete steps that you can take to build your own conceptual framework for your thesis (see also Figure 7.1):

1. Identify the **most important concepts or variables**. Your research question will be a good starting point here (see Chapter 5), but you might also have found further related concepts or variables during the work on your *Literature Review* (or in your data, if you are using a grounded theory approach). Provide clear definitions for your concepts or variables.
2. Try to think about **how these concepts or variables are related to each other**. Again, the existing literature, and in particular existing theories, could help you identify or make such connections.
3. Clearly describe the relationship between the concepts or variables, either in the form of **written hypotheses** (e.g. *"The higher A is, the greater the chance that B occurs"*) or as a **diagram** (e.g. with boxes linked with arrows that show which variables are influencing each other).

Even if you use a diagram for your conceptual model, it makes sense to **explain the relationships between the key variables in written form**, too. Which variables have a positive or negative effect on others, and why? What links can you establish between the variables, and why? Use prior literature (both empirical results and theories) to support your arguments.

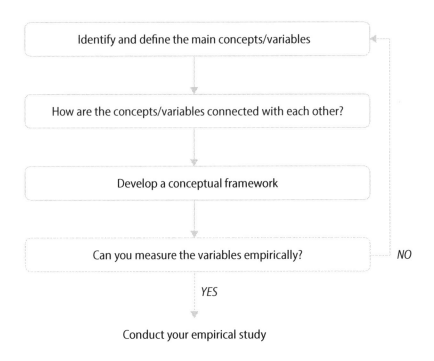

Figure 7.1 Creating a conceptual framework

Let's look at an example. Suppose that our research question is the following:

"How should internal communication in an organization be structured in order to positively influence the organizational commitment of the employees?"

There are two main concepts here: *organizational commitment* and *internal communication*. Organizational commitment can already be considered a **variable**, as it is possible to measure the level of organizational commitment, for example with a survey among the employees of a particular organization. Internal communication is a **concept** (an abstract idea, in this case about certain types of activities within an organization) rather than a variable.

We can now start to think about potential variables that we can use to describe and measure the concept. In this particular case, we could, for example, measure the frequency of communication between managers and employees, the direction of the communication (one-way communication versus a dialogue), or the contents of the communication (e.g. professional topics versus personal issues).

As a next step, once we have identified the key variables that are linked to our research question, we can think about how they are potentially connected with each other. Of course, we could just use our own thoughts and experiences here. Ideally, however, we will also take a look at the literature and see whether we can find theories and research that provide empirical and theoretical support for the proposed links.

Maybe we will find empirical studies that suggest dialogue leads to a higher level of employee commitment than one-way communication, or a theory which proposes that more frequent communication between managers and their team members, including conversations about non-work-related topics, can foster organizational commitment.

We can now either form written hypotheses or create a diagram of our conceptual framework. A **hypothesis** is a concise statement that you can test (i.e. either support or falsify) with empirical data. It is formulated based on the current knowledge in the field, and suggests a relationship between variables that you expect for a certain population of people, objects, or events.

In our example, we could come up with the following hypotheses:

Hypothesis 1: Using dialogic communication instead of one-way communication increases the likelihood that the communication has a positive effect on the organizational commitment of employees.

Hypothesis 2: When managers are communicating about both personal and professional topics with their team members (instead of just professional topics), this increases the likelihood that the communication has a positive effect on the organizational commitment of employees.

Hypothesis 3: More frequent communication between managers and employees increases the likelihood that the communication has a positive effect on the organizational commitment of employees.

Alternatively (or additionally), we could also create a simple **diagram of the conceptual framework** (see the example in Figure 7.2).

Figure 7.2 An example of a graphical conceptual framework

If you have developed your conceptual framework based on the literature, then you can use it as a starting point for your empirical work. Let the framework guide your study.

As a next step, think about how you could **measure the variables** and links that you described in your framework. If you are unable to measure them, it might make sense to circle back and redefine your variables.

 **Tip!**

When trying to build your conceptual framework (or any theory), you do not need to reinvent the wheel. It is possible (and in the eyes of many thesis advisors even necessary) to build your arguments on established theories. You will always have to provide good reasons for why you propose that certain concepts or variables are connected to each other in a specific way. Established theories, especially those that have already been empirically supported, can be very useful for that purpose.

Maybe you could also find and apply theories from outside your immediate research domain. If you are attempting to study the sustainability-related behavior of managers, for example, you could take a look at theories from cognitive psychology, political sciences (power structures in an organization may play a role here), neuroscience (how thought processes influence our sustainability-related behavior), or human geography (how our attachment to places influences sustainability-related behavior). Dare to take a look beyond disciplinary boundaries, and you could be rewarded with highly interesting new insights.

How variables can be related to each other

As we've already discussed, one of the main features of a good conceptual framework or theory is that it explains **how different concepts or variables are related to each other**.

In a thesis, it is very important to be specific about the nature of the suggested relationship between concepts or variables. A particular relationship could be, for example:

- A **correlation**, meaning that the concepts or variables tend to occur or vary together (without implying causality).
- A **causal relationship**, meaning that one variable is seen as the cause of the other variable (the variable you think is the cause is called the *independent variable*; the variable being affected is the *dependent variable*).
- A **mediating relationship**, when variable A influences variable B via (or through) variable C. That means that there is no direct causal effect between A and B, but an indirect one in which A influences C, and C in turn influences B. For example, you might observe that people with a higher income tend to live longer. This is not a direct effect (income does not automatically prolong your life), but an indirect one with access to better health care as a potential *mediator variable*.[3]
- A **moderating relationship**, in which the strength of the relationship between two variables is influenced by a third variable (the *moderator variable*). For example, you might find that the relationship between learning hours per week and the time that people take to reach a certain predefined proficiency in a language course is moderated by age (i.e. people at a lower age need fewer hours to reach the target level than people at a higher age).

Figure 7.3 shows how direct causal relationships, and mediating and moderating relationships, are usually illustrated in graphical form.

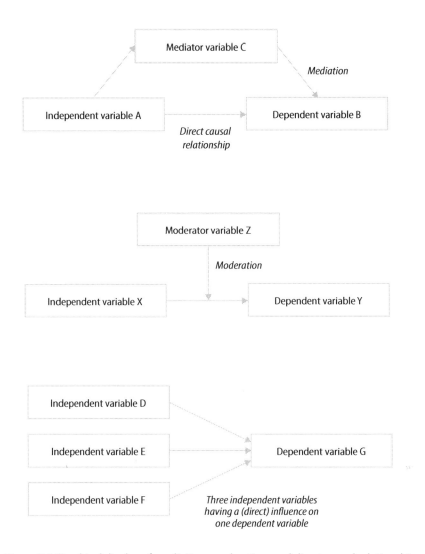

Figure 7.3 Graphical display of mediating, moderating, and direct causal relationships between variables

To complicate things further, there are also different forms of causal relationships:[4]

- The *sufficient condition* ("If there is A, then there will always be B.")
- The *necessary condition* ("B does not exist if A is not present.")
- The *deterministic relation* ("If A is higher, then B is higher.")
- The *probabilistic relation* ("If A is higher, then it is more likely that B is higher, too.")

It's really important here to be specific when you formulate hypotheses or explain how you think certain concepts or variables are related to each other. "If students drink alcohol the night before an exam, then they will get a negative grade in their exam" (as an example of a sufficient condition) has a completely different meaning to "When students drink alcohol the night before an exam, this increases the chance that they will get a negative grade in their exam" (as an example of a probabilistic relation).

Other forms of conceptual frameworks

In addition to correlation and direct causal, mediated, and moderated relationships between variables, there are other ways that concepts could be related to each other:

- In a **sequence**, there is a certain order in which related concepts follow each other.
- A special type of sequence is a **chronological timeline**, in which events are arranged based on the time when they occurred.
- A sequence becomes a **process** (which can be illustrated with a process model) when a series of steps or actions leads to a certain result.
- Concepts can also be clustered into **categories** when they share certain characteristics.

Figure 7.4 shows how these types of conceptual frameworks could be presented in graphical form.

How to write about your conceptual framework in your thesis

Once you've developed your conceptual framework, you'll want to write about it in your thesis, either at the end of the *Literature Review* or in the *Discussion*.

For each **hypothesis** that you develop, summarize a few compelling arguments that you derive from your *Literature Review* (based on both existing theory and empirical research) before you state your hypothesis as a logical outcome of these arguments. Here's a short example:

> *Several theories of motivation consider whether challenging tasks are a key factor in motivating people in a work context. One example is social cognitive theory (Bandura & Locke, 2003), which postulates that challenging goals create a discrepancy which people then want to reduce with goal-oriented behavior. Goal-setting theory also argues that challenging goals motivate people at work (Locke & Latham, 1990). In addition, there is ample empirical support for the motivational effects of challenges, for example in the following studies: [...]. This has also been confirmed in the context of the public sector in research by [...].*

Based on these theoretical and empirical findings, the following is proposed:

Hypothesis 1: If workers in the public sector perceive their work as challenging, it is more likely that they report a higher degree of motivation at work.

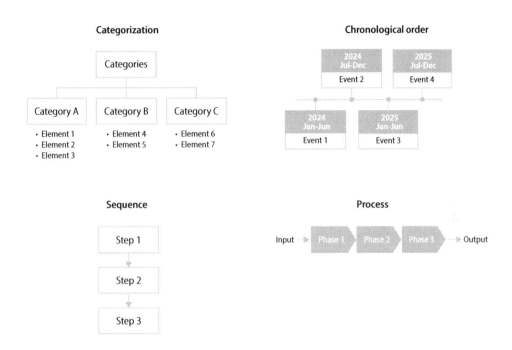

Figure 7.4 Graphical representations of alternative types of conceptual frameworks

The approach will usually be a bit different when you have created a **graphical representation of your theoretical framework**. In this case, it's better to include the diagram first, and then add a few paragraphs that explain the relationships of the concepts or variables in the diagram with arguments based on theory and empirical research. For example:

The conceptual framework presented in Figure X summarizes the key findings from the review of the literature about factors that motivate workers in the public sector.

The first motivational factor is challenging tasks. Several theories of motivation argue that challenging tasks are a key factor for motivating people in a work context. One example is social cognitive theory (Bandura & Locke, 2003) [...].

The second motivational factor is the feeling of contributing to an important cause. [...]

The third motivational factor is [...]

The resulting conceptual framework about work motivation in the public sector forms the basis for the empirical part of this thesis, which is presented in the next two chapters.

Regardless of whether you've chosen to work with written hypotheses or a graphical conceptual framework, make sure that you always include and justify the main arguments that you're basing your framework on (with links to prior literature).

 Thesis writing summary #7

- Use a **conceptual framework as a lynchpin between your *Literature Review* and your empirical work**. Include the main variables that you are studying and the relationships between them. You can use a diagram or written hypotheses (or a combination of both).
- Take three steps to **create your own conceptual framework**: 1. identify the most important concepts or variables, 2. think about how they are related to each other, and 3. describe the relationship in a clear and specific way.
- If you are required to **develop a theory** (which is more often the case in doctoral theses), be sure to add crystal-clear definitions of concepts and variables, and compelling arguments (based on prior knowledge and theories) about why the variables are related to each other in the way that you propose.
- Be exact in **describing the relationship between variables**. Are you trying to find out whether there is a correlation or a causal relationship in the data, or a direct, mediating, or moderating relationship? Or are you interested in whether there's a particular sequence of events or a categorization of elements? A clear description of the connections and relationships that you are studying can save you a lot of time and headaches later in the process, as it provides you with a great guideline for your empirical work and for the presentation and discussion of your findings.

How to choose and describe your research method

In this chapter, we'll give a quick overview of widely used quantitative and qualitative research methods, as well as some tips on how to choose the right method for your own thesis. We'll also provide guidance on what to include in the *Method* (or *Methodology*) section of your thesis.

Choosing the right research method can make or break your thesis project. Carefully consider your options before making your final choice on which method to use.

Quantitative and qualitative research methods in a nutshell

Some university departments allow students to write solely literature-based theses—check your university guidelines or consult with your thesis advisor to find out if this is an option for you. But in most cases, you will be required to conduct **empirical research**, which means that you need to collect and then analyze and interpret data (or "evidence") about the phenomenon that you are interested in.

There are two basic approaches to conducting empirical research: **quantitative** and **qualitative**. The two approaches differ:

- in the **kind of data** you will use (quantifiable, numerical data in the case of quantitative research, and non-numerical data such as text or pictures in qualitative research), and
- in the **methods for analyzing and interpreting the data** (usually statistical methods in quantitative research, and coding and theme-building/categorization methods in qualitative research).

Another distinction is the **purpose of the research**.

Quantitative methods are generally used for measuring and explaining the **relationship between different variables**. In this case, you would typically start with hypotheses about how certain variables are connected to each other (see Chapter 7). Then you would try to collect suitable numerical data that can help you test your hypotheses.

Quantitative research can answer questions like "How many …?", "What is the relationship between X and Y?", "What is the difference between X and Y?", and "What is the effect of X on Y?"

An example of quantitative research would be a study that examines the relationship between alcohol consumption and the risk of liver damage. Another example is testing the hypothesis that private tutoring has a significant positive effect on the average school grades of 8–10-year-old pupils.

You can collect data for quantitative research yourself (e.g. through a survey or structured observations), or you can use secondary data from already published sources.

Table 8.1 provides an overview of different types of quantitative research.

Method	What it is	Example
Descriptive research	Describing the characteristics of a situation or a certain group (e.g. finding out how often something occurs) without determining cause-and-effect relationships	Describing the health-related habits of students (nutrition, exercise)
Correlational research	Trying to find out about the relationship between two (or more) variables, testing the likelihood that these variables occur together (without determining cause-and-effect relationships)	Determining the strength of the relationship between health-related habits of students and their self-reported levels of tiredness in class
Quasi-experimental research	Trying to determine cause-and-effect relationships, often in a natural setting, without being able to control all variables and randomly allocate groups	Studying the effect of using an innovative teaching method with one group of students (the intervention group) on the motivation of students, using a control group that is still taught in a traditional way by the same lecturer in comparison. Although the researcher tries to find two very similar groups (e.g. in terms of age, gender, or prior grades) for the quasi-experiment, it is not possible to randomly assign students to the two classes

Method	What it is	Example
Experimental research	Trying to determine cause-and-effect relationships under controlled conditions in which all subjects are randomly assigned to different groups	A researcher randomly assigns one half of a sample of 120 psychology students to write a few sentences about the pleasure of eating sweets. The other half is requested to write a few sentences about the negative effects on their health of eating sweets. 15 minutes later, both groups of students are offered the same sweets. The researcher tries to find out whether and to what extent consciously thinking about the positive or negative effects of eating sweets can affect actual sweet-eating behavior

Table 8.1 Different types of quantitative research[1]

Qualitative research is usually more focused on **exploring, describing, and understanding the meaning of certain phenomena** (especially in areas that are not yet well understood). When you conduct qualitative research, you will typically try to find themes or patterns in the data, from which you could then derive some kind of theory about why something is happening.

"Why?", "How?", and "In what way?" questions are best answered with the help of qualitative research.

Examples of qualitative research include a study about why a certain student population consumes alcohol, or a study that tries to understand what tutors actually do to improve the learning outcomes of 8–10-year-old pupils.

There's a range of different types of qualitative research. Table 8.2 provides an overview of some of the more common ones. For each method, you can use different **sources of data**, for example:

- **interviews** with experts or members of the group that you intend to study
- **focus groups**, in which a small group of people shares opinions on a certain topic in a moderated setting
- **observations** (including field notes)
- various types of **documents** (e.g. text, pictures, audio, video).

Method	What it is	Example
Phenomenology	Describing certain experiences from the perspective of those who are experiencing it	Research about how certain leadership behaviors have motivating or demotivating effects on team members (based on interviews with team members)
Grounded theory	Collecting data about a phenomenon, and (without preconceived theories) trying to find patterns, concepts, and theories that emerge from the data	Understanding decision-making processes in top management teams through a combination of observations and interview data
Ethnography	Trying to understand the characteristics of the culture of a certain group of people, usually through becoming a participant and immersing oneself in the culture, and then observing and interacting with the people within that culture	Describing the characteristics of the corporate culture in a start-up company
Case study research	An in-depth study of one person, event, process, group, or organization in a real-world context (usually based on different sources, e.g. a combination of multiple interviews, observations and documents); multiple case study designs in which several cases are observed are possible, too	Based on four case studies of students who dramatically improved their language skills, trying to find out which factors contributed to their improvement using interviews with the students, their parents, their teachers, and their tutors, as well as a review of their test results
Content analysis	A systematic analysis of the type and frequency of certain concepts, themes, words, or other types of content in documents (e.g. in text, pictures, audio or video files)	Comparing the contents of sustainability reports of food processing companies based in Germany and the USA
Historical research	Describing events that happened in the past and trying to draw conclusions about their causes, as well as about their effects on the present (and potentially also the future)	Understanding the leadership style of Napoleon Bonaparte and what today's leaders could learn from it

Table 8.2 Different types of qualitative research[2]

You could potentially combine quantitative and qualitative methods in a **mixed methods** (or **multiple methods**) study. For example, you could first use a qualitative study among 10 to 20 consumers to better understand their buying motives for a certain product, and then follow up with a quantitative study with a few hundred participants to get a more accurate picture of the distribution of these buying motives within a certain population. It is also possible to use quantitative methods for analyzing qualitative data, or to include open questions (that reap qualitative data) in a "quantitative" survey.

Another approach to research, which is sometimes used in thesis projects, is **action research**, in which practitioners use qualitative or quantitative research methods to investigate and try to improve their own practice.[3]

Some thesis advisors require you to be specific about which research paradigm you are following in your research. A paradigm is a philosophical way of seeing the world. If you follow a *positivistic paradigm*, you believe that knowledge should be gained and expanded by observing and measuring what is happening in the "real world." Positivistic researchers are usually fans of quantitative methods. If you follow a *constructivist paradigm* instead, you believe that knowledge is always "constructed" through human experience, and is fully dependent on context. Qualitative approaches without preconceived hypotheses are usually the method of choice for researchers who follow the constructivist paradigm. Most researchers, however, prefer to take a pragmatic approach and choose a method that is the "best fit" for answering their research question.

Choosing your method

As you can see from Tables 8.1 and 8.2, there's quite a menu of different research methods you can choose from. So how do you find the right one for your own research project? The following three questions should help you make the right choice:[4]

1. Which method is the **best fit for answering your research question** and achieving your research goal?
2. Which method conforms with the **"norms" of your discipline** and the **expectations of your advisor**?
3. Which method is **practical and feasible for you**, considering your access to data, time and financial constraints, and the research skills that you already have or would still like to develop?

Let's go through these three questions one by one.

Which method is the best fit for achieving your research goal?

First, it is essential to **understand your research goals**. Start by taking a look at the purpose statement for your research again (revisit Chapter 5 if you haven't written one yet). Then go through the various types of quantitative and qualitative research methods in Tables 8.1 and 8.2 and evaluate which method could be a good fit for answering your research question. As a rule of thumb, quantitative methods are usually better for **testing hypotheses and theories** about how certain things are connected with each other, while qualitative methods are preferable for **exploratory research**, in which you try to gain a deeper understanding of certain phenomena (e.g. thought patterns, experiences, or processes) and develop new theories.

Consider the following example: you are interested in what companies in a certain industry do to attract young talent. You could either do quantitative research with a survey that you distribute among human resource managers in the industry, or conduct qualitative case study research in which you explore the talent management practices of selected companies in more detail. If you have already developed a literature-based theory about what companies can do to successfully attract young talent, you would probably go for a quantitative method to test that theory. If you would first like to explore and understand how the process of talent acquisition works, the qualitative option might be the better choice.

Which method conforms with your discipline's "norms" and your advisor's expectations?

Read research papers in your chosen field to find out what methods are typically used for collecting and analyzing data. Skimming through a handful of empirical research articles in your chosen field of research can give you a good feel for the "norms" of your discipline. That does not necessarily mean you need to conform to these norms: using a new method could be exactly the "original contribution" that is often demanded in research, especially at a doctoral level. Seeing the methods that others have used, however, can be an effective way of getting ideas about how you could approach your own research task.

More important than the "norms" of the discipline are actually the expectations of your **thesis advisor**. Once you have an idea of the method you want to use, make sure to check with your advisor before making a final choice.

Which method is practical and feasible for you?

There are also **practical considerations** to take into account when deciding if your preferred method is actually feasible:[5]

- **What data will you have access to?** The method that you choose will be dependent on the nature of the data that you will be able to collect. If you would like to do case study research about decision-making processes in a certain organization, for example, will the decision makers be willing to give you an interview? (Maybe you would want to ask them beforehand.) If you are planning to conduct a survey, try to find out how many people you need in your sample to get statistically significant results (see Chapter 10 for more details). Will you be able to contact enough people in your target population, bearing in mind that often only a small percentage of those you contact will complete the survey? You might also consider working with data that is already available (e.g. analyzing published company annual reports, data that is available through national statistical offices or international organizations, or historical documents). In any case, before you make your decision on the research method, think about what data you require (and in what amount) and how you will get it.
- **How much time and money will you need to conduct your research?** Estimate how much time it will take you to collect and analyze data, and compare that to the time that is available for your empirical work. Quantitative research is usually faster to process than qualitative research, for example, if the latter involves transcribing interview data and going through elaborate coding and pattern recognition procedures (see Chapter 9). How much time you need will also depend on the amount of data you plan to collect and analyze. Try to come to a good estimate here, and don't forget to factor in some time for unforeseen complications, which arise quite often. You might also want to consider costs, for example for traveling, getting access to specific databases, or using special data analysis software.
- **Which research skills would you like to develop?** You likely don't yet have all the skills and knowledge that you need to conduct your research—after all, developing these skills is one of the main reasons for writing a thesis in the first

place. So ask yourself which research skills you would like to develop further. Are you more interested in learning how to analyze numerical data or texts? Do you already have some knowledge of specific software, for example, that you could use? Which method could you also use in future, e.g. in the type of job that you aspire to work in?

When considering all of these points, don't fall into the trap that we often observe: the **tendency to quickly reject quantitative methods** because of "all that complicated statistical stuff." Think twice before you jump to that conclusion! Quantitative data analysis can be a lot easier than you think (especially compared to qualitative analysis methods). There are tried-and-tested methods for which you can find step-by-step instructions in textbooks or online. In most cases, you won't need to do statistical calculations yourself—there are great software packages available that can do this work for you. You will just need to learn how to use them and how to interpret the results correctly.

The most **challenging parts of quantitative research** are usually developing a suitable research instrument (e.g. a questionnaire) and getting access to a high number of contacts in your target population (if you are conducting a survey). The two **main challenges of qualitative research**, on the other hand, are getting access to the right people in order to conduct suitable interviews and the rather complex and time-consuming data analysis methods.

So whichever direction you take, there's no "easy way out." The right question for finding your method is probably not "What do I want to avoid?" but "Where can I learn the most?"

Writing the *Method* section

Once you have chosen and implemented your method, you will then have to describe it in detail in the *Method* (or *Methodology* or *Research Methodology*) chapter of your thesis. You can think of this chapter as being like a cooking recipe. When someone else follows this recipe, they should be able to replicate your study.[6]

Here's what is usually included in the *Method* chapter:

1. **The research question and purpose of your research.** You can restate them here even if you have already presented them in the *Introduction*.
2. **The method that you selected and a rationale for why you consider it the best method** for answering your research question.
3. **The population and sample of your research.** "Population" refers to the entire group that you would like your conclusions to be applicable for, while "sample" is the part of that group you will actually collect data from (see Figure 8.1). You

should also describe your sampling procedure, providing information about the criteria with which you selected your sample. More information about an optimal sample size and different sampling procedures is provided in Chapters 9 (for qualitative research) and 10 (for quantitative research).

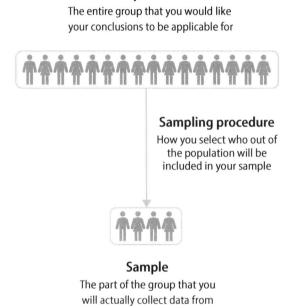

Population
The entire group that you would like
your conclusions to be applicable for

Sampling procedure
How you select who out of
the population will be
included in your sample

Sample
The part of the group that you
will actually collect data from

Figure 8.1 Population and sample

4. **Instruments that you used for collecting data** (e.g. a questionnaire or an observation guideline). Ideally, you will be able to use tried-and-tested instruments (e.g. certain scales that have been used before in psychological research). If tried-and-tested instruments are not available, you will have to explain how you developed your own instrument (e.g. through a pilot study). Describe what is being measured and how you measured it.
5. **Data collection**—including when and where you collected the data, and all the steps that you took to get all the data that you need.
6. **Ethical considerations**—especially linked to the protection of human subjects (e.g. what you did to ensure privacy and confidentiality, or to get consent for participation in the research).

7. **Data analysis**—with a detailed explanation of which statistical methods were chosen and why (in the case of quantitative research), or of the coding, theme-building, and categorization methods you are using to make sense of the data in a structured way (in the case of qualitative research). The *Method* chapter doesn't include the data analysis itself yet, but just a description and justification of the methods used to analyze the data. You will present the results of your data analysis in your *Results* chapter (see Chapter 11).

8. **Measures for ensuring research quality**—including *reliability* ("consistency" or "repeatability," so that you would get the same results if you—or someone else—repeated the research), *validity* ("correctness" in the sense that you are really measuring what you want to measure), and *objectivity* (minimizing the influence of the researcher's personal biases).

There are different approaches to ensuring reliability, validity, and objectivity for different research methods. One way to ensure reliability in quantitative research is to use different questions about the same issue, and then check whether the respondents answer these questions in a consistent way (e.g. with the help of the statistical measure Cronbach's alpha). In case study research, reliability can be enhanced by compiling a case study database, in which all documents collected during the study are stored, and a case study protocol, which includes all the detailed steps of how the research has been conducted. A book or website about your chosen research method will give you more detailed information about how to ensure you meet relevant research quality criteria.

There's hardly any other decision you'll make that has a bigger influence on your chances of succeeding with your thesis project than the choice of the right research method. The following two chapters will provide you with additional insights into qualitative and quantitative research methods, so you might also want to take a look at them before making your final decision.

Thesis writing summary #8

- **Familiarize yourself with different research methods.** Quantitative methods are generally used for measuring relationships between different variables, and qualitative methods for gaining an in-depth understanding of certain phenomena or developments. Within these broader categories, there are more specific methods that you can choose from.
- **Make sure there is a good fit between your research purpose and the research method.** Do you want to test theories? Compare certain groups of people or concepts? Or try to understand how one variable influences another? Then you will probably want to consider quantitative methods. For answering questions that start with "Why?", "How?", or "In what way?", take a look at qualitative methods first.
- **Take inspiration from prior work in the field.** Read the *Method* part of research papers in your area of interest, and see what you can learn from them.
- **Consider practical constraints when you choose your research methods.** Most importantly, consider which data you will have access to, and don't forget to think about potential constraints regarding time, money, and the efforts needed to develop the required research skills and knowledge.
- **Write the *Method* section of your thesis like a cooking recipe.** If another person follows all the steps that you include in the *Method* section, they should be able to replicate your study. Make sure to include your chosen method (and your rationale for selecting it), information about the population, sample, and sampling procedure, data collection (including the instruments that you used), ethical considerations, data analysis procedures, and what you have done to ensure research quality.

How to conduct qualitative research

Qualitative research is all about collecting and analyzing non-numerical data. Students often analyze **texts** in their thesis project (e.g. interview transcripts, field notes, news articles, social media posts, reports, diary entries, or open-ended responses from surveys), but qualitative data also includes **pictures** as well as **audio and video sources**.

As we have already discussed in Chapter 8, there's a range of **general methodological approaches in qualitative research**, including:

- **phenomenology:** describing experiences from the perspective of those who are experiencing it
- **grounded theory:** developing theories based on patterns that emerge from the data without any preconceived theories
- **ethnography:** trying to understand a culture through immersing yourself in it)
- **case study research:** with the aim of gaining an in-depth understanding of a phenomenon in a real-life context
- **content analysis:** systematically analyzing the frequency of certain contents in documents
- **historical research:** trying to draw conclusions from how events unfolded in the past.

It's beyond the scope of this book to describe all of these approaches in detail. We therefore recommend you take a look at **books about qualitative research and qualitative data analysis** to find more detailed instructions about how to use a specific method.

**Tip!**

You can find more detailed information about qualitative research methods in the following books that are fully dedicated to this topic, for example:

- *Qualitative Research: A Guide to Design and Implementation* by Sharan Merriam and Elizabeth Tisdall and *Qualitative Research Design: An Interactive Approach* by Joseph A. Maxwell both provide a good overview on how to plan and implement a qualitative research study.
- *Qualitative Data Analysis: A Methods Sourcebook* by Matthew Miles, A. Michael Huberman and Johnny Saldaña is a great resource that includes "how-to" advice on lots of different methods for coding, analyzing and displaying qualitative data.
- Robert Yin's *Case Study Research and Applications* is a classic introductory text to case study research.
- If you're considering content analysis as your method of choice for analyzing qualitative data, you might want to take a look at Philipp Mayring's *Qualitative Content Analysis: A Step-by-Step Guide*.

Regardless of which method you choose, however, this chapter will give you an overview of what you will typically need to consider in your qualitative research work.

Sampling in qualitative research

A major decision to be made in any type of empirical research is what (or who) to include in your **sample**.

While in quantitative research the aim of **sampling** is to select subjects that are statistically representative of a larger group (the "population"), sampling in qualitative research is more about identifying and selecting "information-rich cases related to the phenomenon of interest."[1] The "cases" could, for example, be people, events, or organizations. Instead of statistical generalization, the aim is usually **analytic generalization**, which means that the theoretical inferences that you are drawing from the data are also applicable to similar cases or situations.

In qualitative research, a typical sampling procedure begins with the definition of a **"target population"** or a **"sample universe"**—that's all of the cases which potentially qualify for inclusion in the study. You can define both **inclusion criteria** and

exclusion criteria to clarify which cases could generally be part of the sample universe.[2] The sample universe also defines the totality of cases that the findings of your study should eventually be applicable to.

There's a range of different **sampling methods** for qualitative research. Examples include:[3]

- **typical case sampling:** selecting "average" cases that are "typical" for the sample universe
- **outlier/extreme case sampling:** selecting very unusual cases (e.g. extremely successful companies, or cases of "extreme" failure)
- **maximum variation sampling:** selecting cases which differ considerably for certain characteristics (useful to find out whether there are differences between different groups of cases)
- **purposive sampling:** including cases that are likely to be most informative regarding the research purpose (e.g. interviewing individuals who are highly experienced or knowledgeable in a field)
- **theoretical sampling** (often used in grounded theory studies): selecting cases that best represent emerging theoretical concepts
- **criterion sampling:** including cases that match certain predefined (inclusion and/or exclusion) criteria.

One of the most difficult questions in qualitative research is how many cases to include in your study. There's no general "right" answer here, as the issue of **sample size** in qualitative research remains "the subject of enduring discussions."[4] "How many" depends on a range of different factors, including the type of method that you use (case study research usually requires a smaller sample than, for example, the analysis of expert interviews), the homogeneity or heterogeneity of the group you are studying (smaller samples are needed for more homogeneous groups), and pragmatic considerations like resources and time constraints or the volume of data that you collect per case.

A key idea for determining sample size in qualitative research is the principle of **saturation** (also called "theoretical saturation" in a grounded theory context). It means that you should add more cases until you reach a point where you won't get further relevant knowledge out of additional cases—there are no new insights, ideas, coding categories, or themes emerging from the new cases that you haven't already noticed. When using interviews as a data source, an often-cited rule of thumb for what is needed to reach the point of saturation is that if there is "a shared perception, belief, or behavior among a relatively homogeneous group, then a sample of twelve will likely be sufficient."[5]

One way to "measure" saturation is to count the number of new categories or themes that emerge from each additional case that you are analyzing. Let's assume, for example, that you are trying to analyze what kind of social and environmental sustainability initiatives are set by retail companies (e.g. through analyzing their sustainability reports). You could, for example, use a table to note down during your coding process (see page 100) how many new categories of initiatives emerged from each additional interview. From Table 9.1, you can see that there were no new categories of social or environmental initiatives to be found after case 7, which is an indication that a point of saturation has been reached.

Case number	1	2	3	4	5	6	7	8	9
New categories of social initiatives	3	2	3	2	1	1	-	-	-
New categories of environmental initiatives	4	2	2	1	2	-	1	-	-

Table 9.1 Example of a table to determine the point of saturation for a qualitative study

The only real "universal" guideline for determining sample size is to discuss it with your thesis advisor: they should be able to help you figure out the best sample size for your specific research demands.

Data collection and interviewing

For some research topics, you will be able to obtain readily available data, such as annual reports that can easily be downloaded from company websites.

However, many students choose to conduct **interviews** for their thesis project, either as the main data source or as one out of several sources in a case study research project where data from various sources are combined.

Arguably the most widely used form of interviews are **semi-structured interviews**. These are based on an interview guide, with a set of predetermined open-ended questions which are complemented with additional questions that emerge from the conversation. Such interviews are typically at least 30 minutes long, and often considerably longer to be able to explore certain topics in adequate depth.[6]

Here are some **tips for preparing your interview guide**:[7]

- Derive the questions from your research question (and sub-questions) and the theoretical framework that you have developed from your literature review (see Chapter 7).
- Keep the questions as simple and easy to understand as possible, and well-adapted to the target group.
- Ask one question at a time (e.g. "When did you introduce the new targets, and what happened next?" would be better split into two separate questions).
- Use open questions and formulate them in a way that will elicit longer answers from your interviewees.
- Think about a "warm-up" question to begin the interview with: something that is relatively easy to answer and can help you to build rapport, but is connected to what you would like to find out so it still generates relevant data.
- Follow a logical progression with your interview questions (e.g. from broader to narrower questions).
- Don't overload the interview guide with questions. It is usually better to focus on a few key questions that are related to your core research questions, and then to use follow-up questions if necessary, than to have a long list of questions that the interviewees become tired of answering.
- Ask questions that tap into the experience of the interviewees and do not let them do the analysis work (that's your job, not theirs!).
- Include an empowering closing question that leaves the interviewee with a positive feeling about the interview, and about you as an interviewer.

When formulating your questions, you should ideally already have some idea in mind about how you would like to analyze the data (see the section on qualitative data analysis on pages 99–107)—that will make your later analysis work much easier.

There are **practicalities** to consider about arranging interviews, too. Some potential interviewees might have very limited time available, or might be difficult to contact in the first place; others might be easier to reach at certain times in the year (teachers and lecturers, for example, may be easier to contact during term time).

You can increase your chances of getting an interview if you try to schedule it well in advance and be flexible regarding when it is held.

When you **ask for an interview**, don't write lengthy, long-winded emails or messages on social media like LinkedIn. Keep your request clear and concise. Write in a personal way, briefly describe the purpose of your research, explain why you want to interview them in particular, and indicate the planned duration of the interview (30 minutes will sound more doable for most people than two hours here). Consider offering anonymity and confidentiality if necessary.

Here is a template for an interview request email.

Re: Invitation to participate in a research project about [...]

Dear [Name],

My name is [...] and I'm currently working on a master's thesis/research project for [...] University, with the aim of increasing our understanding of the influence of [...] on [...].

As you have extensive experience in [...], I would like to ask if you might kindly take part in an interview as part of this research project? It shouldn't take up much more than 30 to 40 minutes of your precious time, and could be held as a phone call or videoconference call.

In the interview I'd like to ask you about [provide a brief list of topics or representative questions]. Of course, I can also ensure confidentiality if needed.

I'd like to suggest September 30th at 8:30am for the interview call, but I can be flexible if another day and time suits you better. Please just let me know what works best for you.

Thank you in advance for considering helping me with my thesis project, and please do not hesitate to ask if you have any further questions!

Best wishes

[Your name]

To increase your chances of getting an interview, try to **phone your potential interviewees** (or leave a voice message) in addition to sending an email or message. There is some effort involved in this, but it's one of the most effective strategies for convincing other people that it is really important for you to talk to them.

You can also send one or two **reminders** after a few days. In exceptional cases, when someone who would be the "perfect" interview partner for you quickly says "no," you could maybe even consider writing a short follow-up email in which you ask them to reconsider and explain why you really need to interview them (but be careful with such follow-up emails; if the potential interviewee refuses once more, don't try again, although you could thank them for their time).

When you use a recording device to record the interviews (only with prior permission from the interviewees, of course), you will then need to **transcribe the recordings.** Check with your thesis advisor as to which type of transcription is required: verbatim (including the "um's" and "ah's") or "intelligent verbatim" (that's a slightly edited version excluding irrelevant filler words and maybe also with some minor grammatical fixes).

Tip!

When you transcribe your interviews:

1. Record the exact place and time of the interview, as well as the name of the interviewer and interviewee.
2. Work in short sequences—listen for 10 to 15 seconds, then type, and re-listen if necessary.
3. Start a new paragraph for each new idea.
4. Once you are finished, listen to the recording again to check the accuracy of your transcription—make edits if necessary as you listen and read through your draft at the same time.
5. If you have a lot of text to transcribe, take a look at AI-powered transcription software (you will find a wide selection if you type "transcription software" into a search engine)—but don't forget to edit the transcript yourself afterwards to ensure it is accurate.

One thing to consider in qualitative research is that data collection can take quite some time, especially if you plan to interview people. So make sure you reserve enough time for this task, and start as early as possible. Remember too that transcribing takes time; a rough estimate is to factor in approximately four hours of transcription time per hour of interview.

To ensure the credibility of your research, it is good practice to **keep detailed records** about all the choices that you are making in the data collection process. In case study research, a detailed guide that includes all steps that you are taking in selecting cases, data collection, and data analysis is called a "**case study protocol.**"

Qualitative data analysis

Completing your data collection is an important milestone in your thesis project. The next challenge is to analyze that data.

You will find plenty of books about qualitative data analysis, and we would recommend you check out one or two of these before you start analyzing your data.

There's also a wide range of different methods that you can use to make sense of qualitative data. But before you get into the detail, let's take a quick look at the **basics of qualitative data analysis**, which typically includes five steps:[8]

1. Familiarize yourself with the data
2. Set a clear focus for your analysis
3. Categorize the data
4. Identify themes, patterns, and connections in the data
5. Interpret and make sense of the data

Step by step, here is how it works.

Step 1—Familiarize yourself with the data

Read and reread (in the case of texts) or look through (in the case of visual or audiovisual data) all the material you have gathered to gain a good overview of what you have. Take notes about anything that you find interesting in relation to your research question. You may already notice some prevalent topics and emerging themes, or connections between the data at this stage.

Step 2—Set a clear focus for your analysis

You will probably have a lot of data in front of you, and not everything will be relevant for answering your research question. Be clear on what you would like to learn from the data, so that you can accomplish your research purpose. One way of focusing your analysis work is to take your research question as a starting point, and then formulate a few key questions that you would like to answer through analyzing the data. These questions can change along the way, but they will help you to set the right priorities from the beginning of your analysis work.[9]

Step 3—Categorize the data

This crucial (and usually quite labor-intensive) step of categorizing qualitative data is also called **coding**. Codes are basically labels that describe "chunks" of data. Let's assume you've found the following sentence in an interview that you conducted with an executive coach:

> *"I find it very challenging if the expectations of the people who I am supposed to coach differ from the expectations of their managers in terms of the purpose and potential outcomes of the coaching intervention."*

A potential code for this chunk of data could be "coaching challenges." You could then assign the same code to other data that relates to coaching challenges. If you are then interested in analyzing all the challenges that executive coaches are faced with, you would just have to look at all chunks of text with the code "coaching challenges" and identify patterns or themes in that particular category of data (in Step 4 of your analysis work—see below).

It is also possible to assign several different codes to one particular chunk of data. Another potential code for the example above could be "expectations." Using the same code across the whole dataset would again enable you to organize into one category all the data that is linked to the expectations that coaches are faced with.

Of course, you do not need to code all your data. You can skip, for example, parts of an interview that go far off-topic. Just focus on coding those parts of the data where the content is potentially relevant for answering your research question.

There are **two basic approaches to coding**: deductive and inductive coding (see Figure 9.1).

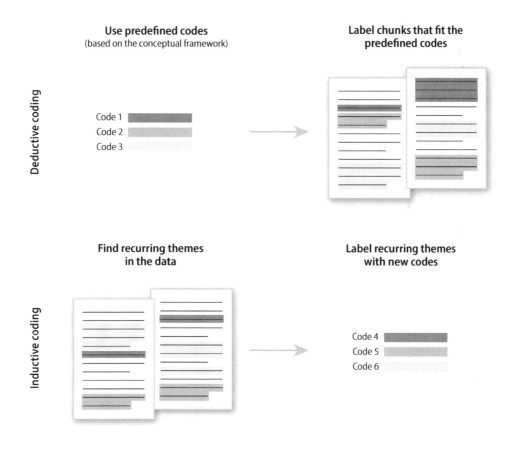

Figure 9.1 Deductive and inductive coding

Deductive (or a priori) coding means that you start coding with a predetermined list of codes, guided by your research questions, theories, or conceptual framework. Creating a list with all the codes you are looking for (a **"codebook"**), neatly organized in categories and sub-categories, allows you to approach the coding task in a very structured way that is clearly linked with your conceptual work.

Inductive (or emergent) coding means that the codes "emerge progressively during data collection."[10] You will develop inductive codes "on the go" when you find recurring themes or issues in the data. These can either be **descriptive codes** (that's when you assign a suitable word or short phrase that describes the key topic in a chunk of qualitative data) or **in vivo codes** (that's using the exact words or short phrases that the interviewees used, e.g. "outcomes of the coaching intervention" in the example above).

It is possible to combine deductive and inductive coding, and in most cases your codebook will also change over time. You can continue to add new codes or change them until no new themes or sub-themes emerge. Some codes may prove to be quite worthless if they turn out not to represent a recurring theme, while others might get too "crowded" with data. In the latter case, it will usually make sense to break the codes down into sub-codes.

When you introduce new codes, you will need to revisit the data that you haven't yet applied the new codes to. This means that during the coding procedure you will have to go through the whole dataset very thoroughly at least twice: once until you have created a coherent codebook (see Table 9.2 for an example), and a second time to make sure that you have applied all the codes from the codebook to the whole dataset.

····· **Tip!** ···

Although it is possible to code manually (e.g. applying different colors to chunks of text to represent the different codes), the process becomes a lot easier with the help of qualitative data analysis software. There are different options here, including MAXQDA, ATLAS.ti, NVivo, QDA Miner, and Dedoose (to name just a few). Check out their websites and offers. Some of them offer trial versions and online tutorials. These tools are usually quite easy to master, and they can help you save a lot of time during your data analysis process.

··

Category: COACHING CHALLENGES (category abbreviation CHA)	Code abbreviation
CHA-COMMUNICATION CHALLENGE	CHA-COMM
CHA-RELATIONSHIP CHALLENGE	CHA-REL
CHA-ORGANIZATIONAL CHALLENGE	CHA-ORG
...	
Category: COACHING BENEFITS (category abbreviation BEN)	**Code abbreviation**
BEN-FOR COACHEES	BEN-C
Self-confidence	BEN-C-SELF
Personal development	BEN-C-DEV
Problem solving	BEN-C-SOLV
Goal attainment	BEN-C-GOAL
Learning	BEN-C-LEAR
...	
BEN-FOR THE ORGANIZATION	BEN-O
Higher work productivity	BEN-O-PROD
Return on investment	BEN-O-ROI
...	

Table 9.2 Example of an excerpt of a codebook

Step 4—Identify themes, patterns, and connections in the data

Once you have organized your data with the help of codes, you can start looking for patterns. If you extract the chunks of text with the code COACHING CHALLENGES in the example above (qualitative data analysis software will usually allow you to export code-related data, for example into Excel files), you can try to identify patterns in the challenges that executive coaches experience.

Such patterns could include:

- **common themes** that you can find in the data
- **similarities and differences** (e.g. for different groups of respondents)
- **outliers** that you can learn something from (e.g. is there anything that runs counter to the prevailing themes?)
- the **relative importance of certain themes** (when some themes appear a lot more often than others)
- **relationships between themes** (data items or codes that always occur together, in a sequence, as sub-categories of a broader category, or in a cause–effect relationship).

There are several ways you can find such patterns. You could, for example, just read through all the text extracts that are associated with one code and then provide a **narrative description** of the patterns you can identify. This involves summarizing the main points that you find in the data—what are the key similarities and differences in that particular category?

Most thesis advisors will expect you to go beyond simply writing narrative descriptions, however, and expect you to use more sophisticated **data condensation** and **data display** methods.

First, let's take a look at **data condensation methods**. You could, for example, condense text data with the help of a table in which you gradually reduce the original data with the aim of extracting its essence (see Table 9.3 for an example).

Interview no.	Text excerpt	Reduction	Generaliza-tion	Code applied
5	*"I find it very challenging if the expectations of the people who I am supposed to coach differ from the expectations of their managers in terms of the purpose and potential outcomes of the coaching intervention."*	Challenge: different expectations of coaches and managers	Challenge: diverging expectations	CHA-REL
...	...	...	...	...

Table 9.3 An example of a data reduction table

Another example of data condensation is to group together codes with similar themes, and reduce these down into overarching themes (see Figure 9.2 for an example).

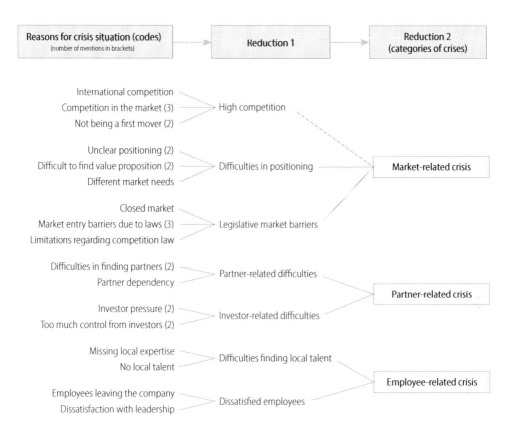

Figure 9.2 From codes to categories: example of a multiple-step condensation/categorization process (adapted from a student thesis about organizational crises in high-growth start-up companies)[11]

Two widely used forms of **data display** are matrices and networks. A **matrix display** is a way of condensing material into a chart or table so that you can spot the patterns "at a glance."[12] Miles, Huberman and Saldaña in their highly recommended book *Qualitative Data Analysis* propose a wide range of different matrices for qualitative data analysis. Examples include an **event-listing matrix**, in which events in several categories are chronologically arranged (see Table 9.4), and a **cross-case analysis matrix**, which presents relevant (reduced) data on several variables of interest from multiple cases in a structured way (see Table 9.5).[13]

		Time period			
		Oct–Dec 2023	Jan–Mar 2023	Apr–Jun 2023	Jul–Sep 2023
Level of analysis	Society	(Reduced) data	…		
	Organization	…			
	Team				
	Individual				

Table 9.4 Example of an event-listing matrix

		Variables			
		Variable 1	Variable 2	Variable 3	Variable 4
Cases	Case A	Data	…		
	Case B	…			
	Case C				
	Case D				

Table 9.5 Example of cross-case analysis matrix

Network displays are another common way of presenting qualitative data. They consist of labeled nodes connected by lines or arrows. They are a great way of showing how different concepts are connected to each other (see Figure 9.3).

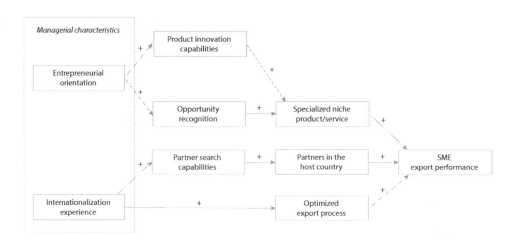

Figure 9.3 Example of a network display showing the determinants of the export performance of small- and medium-sized enterprises

These are just a few examples of methods that you can use for data analysis. Whatever method (or combination of methods) you eventually apply, make sure that you take a **systematic approach** to analyzing your data, and present your data in such a way that the patterns you would like to highlight become clearly visible.

Remember to keep track of all the steps that you are taking during the analysis process so that others are able to follow your reasoning—this will make your research and its results more credible.[14]

 **Tip!**

Instead of identifying and clustering themes in a thematic analysis, you could use a content analysis approach to extract meaning from your qualitative data. The aim of content analysis (or "conceptual analysis") is to determine the number of times certain concepts (e.g. words, themes, pictures) are present in a particular dataset. You could, for example, check how many times certain words or themes occur in the last 300 social media posts of a certain organization, or how often the pictures in those posts featured people of different genders, ages, or ethnicities. That would be a very simple form of content analysis.[15]

Step 5—Interpret and make sense of the data

Finally, once you have structured the data and identified themes, patterns, and connections, it is time to pose and answer the question *"So what?"*

What have you learned from the data? How does it help you to answer your research question? Summarize your main findings in a few key points, and report your insights in a concise way.

Quality criteria for qualitative research

When you conduct (and report on) qualitative research, there are a few quality criteria to consider:[16]

- **Credibility:** is the data accurately representing the phenomenon that you are attempting to study? This is similar to *internal validity* in quantitative research (see Chapter 10). Credibility can be enhanced, for example, with triangulation (cross-checking data using different sources, e.g. asking different members of a team about team processes, or checking whether documents confirm what people said in interviews), or member checks (getting feedback on your interpretations from participants in the study).

- **Transferability:** the extent to which the results can be transferred to other cases or situations—similar to *external validity* or *generalizability* in quantitative research. It can be ensured, for example, by applying purposive sampling based on clear selection criteria and using "thick descriptions" that provide detailed background information about the context of the research.
- **Dependability:** the potential for the study to be replicated—similar to *reliability* in quantitative research. This can be enhanced through creating an audit trail (e.g. a detailed protocol of the decisions that you have taken in the research process) or using outside reviewers (as a graduate student, this would be your thesis or dissertation committee).
- **Confirmability:** ensuring the results are not biased by either the researcher or participants—similar to *objectivity* in quantitative research. This can be enhanced with triangulation and practicing reflexivity (being aware of and explicitly reporting on potential biases).

Be sure to report on what steps you took in the *Method* section of your thesis. Creating an audit trail through documenting the choices that you make during your research process is necessary for ensuring the quality of your research.

As you can see, there's a lot to consider when you conduct qualitative research. That's why dipping into one (or several) books on qualitative research methods before you start with your data collection and analysis work is always a good idea.

Once you have chosen and familiarized yourself with the right method, a qualitative research project can be a highly rewarding experience. It will enable you to immerse yourself in the experience of other people, learn more about how and why things are happening, and generate rich insights and an in-depth understanding of your research subject.

Thesis writing summary #9 ·····················

- **Decide on your method first.** There are a range of different methodological approaches to qualitative research. Get an overview of them, decide on a method, and familiarize yourself with qualitative data analysis processes and tools before you start immersing yourself in the data.
- **Identify the right sample and sample size.** Use a structured sampling method, set a minimum sample size number (together with your thesis advisor) and then continue to add additional cases (e.g. interviews) until you have reached a point of saturation (where you are confident that you will not get considerably more knowledge out of adding further cases).
- **Collect the data.** You can either use published sources or conduct your own interviews. If you go for interviews, make sure you follow the tips on page 97 for preparing an effective interview guide and think about a strategy to get access to your target group. Keep in mind that this can be one of the most difficult parts of the whole thesis project!
- **Follow the five steps of qualitative data analysis.** 1. Familiarize yourself with the data; 2. Set a clear focus for your analysis; 3. Categorize the data; 4. Identify themes, patterns, and connections in the data; and 5. Interpret and make sense of the data.
- **Ensure the quality of your qualitative research.** Strategies like triangulation (using different sources of data to study a phenomenon) or creating an audit trail with a thorough protocol of your choices during the research process can help to ensure the credibility of your research.

How to conduct quantitative research

Quantitative research is all about **analyzing numerical data** with the help of statistical methods. You can either collect data yourself, for example in a survey, or use existing data from other sources like national statistical offices or international organizations. You could even "convert" qualitative data into quantitative data, for example by counting how often certain elements or categories occur in a qualitative dataset (e.g. taking the annual reports of 50 different corporations and counting the number of times they reference certain categories of sustainable behavior), and then taking the resulting numbers as a basis for statistical analyses.

Many students are put off by the thought of "doing statistics." At first sight, it sounds a bit like having to understand and conduct complex mathematical calculations. But don't worry: taking the quantitative option doesn't mean that you need to be or become a mathematical wizard. If you understand which is the right method to use (and this chapter will help you to choose), then you can let software tools do the number crunching for you.

Your main job is not to make any complicated calculations, but to provide the input data in an adequate form and then to interpret the results. And there is a lot of support out there (e.g. YouTube videos) that can help you master your chosen quantitative method relatively quickly.

There are a number of different quantitative methods available. This again is nothing to worry about, because you don't need to understand all of them but just the one that's right for your research purpose. Regardless of the method that you will finally choose, we will give you some general tips in this chapter about what you need to consider if you decide to go down the "numbers path" in your thesis project.

Tip!

You can find more detailed information about quantitative research methods in books that are fully dedicated to this topic, for example:

- Daniela Aidley's *Introducing Quantitative Methods: A Practical Guide* or Peter Nardi's *Doing Survey Research: A Guide to Quantitative Methods*, which provide a general overview of quantitative methods
- Andy Field's *Discovering Statistics Using IBM SPSS Statistics* or Julie Pallant's *SPSS Survival Manual*, which are both fabulous step-by-step introductions to using the widely used software package IBM SPSS for statistical data analysis. If you use R as an alternative software for data analysis, you can find good guidance in Andy Field, Jeremy Miles and Zoe Field's *Discovering Statistics Using R*
- books that are focused on the application of quantitative methods in specific disciplines, like Les Oakshott's *Essential Quantitative Methods: For Business, Management, and Finance* or Daniel Muijs's *Doing Quantitative Research in Education with IBM SPSS Statistics*.

Let's take a look at a few basics of quantitative research, including **sampling**, developing a **questionnaire**, how to **present your data in tables and charts**, how to **choose the right method for further data analysis**, and how to **ensure the quality** of your quantitative research.

Sampling in quantitative research

In quantitative research, **sampling** is the process of selecting individuals (collectively known as the "**sample**") from a larger group (the "**population**"). The purpose of sampling is to measure and analyze something in the sample, and then generalize the findings from the sample to the population as a whole.

To make this possible, the sample should ideally be **representative** of the population. This means that the sample must closely resemble the population in key characteristics. In a narrower sense, representativeness also means that each individual in the population has had the same chance to become part of the sample.

There are two **basic types of sampling methods**: probability and non-probability sampling.

In **probability sampling**, individuals are randomly selected from the population. This type of sampling meets the representativeness criterion in a narrower sense, as every individual has exactly the same chance of being part of the sample. This type of sampling method is the "strongest" one in terms of then being able to make statistical interferences about the population.

There are four categories of probability sampling:[1]

1. **Simple random sampling:** for example, when you assign the numbers 1 to 1,000 to the 1,000 people that make up a population and then randomly draw 100 numbers to determine your sample.

2. **Systematic sampling:** here you would likewise assign the numbers 1 to 1,000 to the 1,000 people that make up the population, but instead of randomly selecting numbers, you use every n^{th} element on the list to be included in the sample (e.g. every 10th number, so number 10, 20, 30 ...).

3. **Stratified random sampling:** you first divide the population into subsegments (or "strata") that differ on characteristics that are relevant for your research. You then use random sampling to select a sample from each subsegment in the same proportion in which the relevant characteristic is represented in the population. For example, if you are interested in how people with a degree think differently about a certain topic from those who do not hold a degree, and if the overall population includes 300 people with a degree and 700 people without a degree, you would first divide the population into two strata based on whether they hold a degree or not, then randomly select 30 people from the degree strata and 70 people from the non-degree strata to get an overall sample of 100 people.

4. **Cluster sampling:** you also divide the population into subsegments here, but then randomly select whole subsegments instead of individuals from each subsegment. This will only work well, however, if each subsegment has similar characteristics to the entire population. Let's assume, for example, that your population are employees in 30 local subsidiaries of a multinational company. In this case, you could randomly select five of these subsidiaries (the "clusters"), and then try to survey all employees in these five offices. If you are not able to survey everyone, but again use a sampling method to choose who to interview in the five selected offices, you are conducting two-stage (or multiple-stage) sampling.

In **non-probability sampling methods**, we do not know the exact likelihood that each individual will be included in the sample. These type of sampling methods are usually easier to implement, but they also come with a higher risk of sampling bias (when some parts of a population have a higher chance of being included than others), which can lead to limitations for the statistical generalizability of your research results.

The most popular **non-probability sampling methods** are:

1. **Convenience sampling:** here you just take individuals that are easily available into your sample (which is why it's also called an "availability sample"). For example, you could use a social media post to ask some friends or followers to take part in your survey. This might be easy to implement, but the downside is that your results will most probably not be representative of the population you are interested in. In this sense, it can be considered to be the "worst" sampling method.

2. **Quota sampling:** in this case, you first check the distribution of key characteristics in your population and then set quotas for including individuals with those characteristics in the sample. If half of the population is male and the other half female, for example, you would also want half of your sample to be male and half to be female. There are some problems with this type of sampling, in particular the fact that other characteristics (any that have not been used to set the quotas) may not be equally or fairly represented. It also doesn't make sense to set quotas for a sample if you do not know the exact distribution of certain characteristics in the overall population.

3. **Snowball sampling:** this is when you first identify a few people who fully fit your selection criteria, and then let them refer you to other people. This type of sampling can be useful when you are studying a population whose members are difficult to identify "from the outside." As with the two non-probability methods above, representativeness remains rather weak with this method, too.

4. **Purposive sampling:** this is when you use your expertise to select a sample based on a good understanding of the characteristics of the population, making informed judgments (which is why it is also called a "judgmental sample") of which elements the sample must include, so that for purpose of your research it "can be logically assumed to be representative of the population."[2] Make your rationale and choices clear when you use a purposive sample, and acknowledge that it will not be representative of the population in a strict statistical sense.

One of the most burning questions of students who choose a quantitative approach for their thesis project is **"What's the right sample size?"**

The answer is one that you are probably already very familiar with as a student: "It depends." In this case, it depends on

- the **size of the overall population**,
- the **margin of error**, which indicates whether the results of the sample are accurate for the population as a whole; it's a range, expressed in percent-

age points, by which the "true value" in the overall population may deviate from the sample (a +/–5% margin of error is, for example, frequently used in research), and

- the **confidence level** you would like to achieve. The confidence level describes the probability (expressed as a percentage) that your sample will adequately represent the population (95% is often used as a standard confidence level in research).

A combination of these factors determine whether a sample can be considered to be statistically representative of a population or not.

For pros, there are mathematical formulas that can be used to determine your sample size. The rest of us can use a sample size calculator. You should easily be able to find one by typing "sample size calculator" into a search engine.[3]

Developing a questionnaire for quantitative research

Once you've determined your sample, you will need to collect data from it. There are several methods that you can use for collecting quantitative data, for example conducting experiments, recording observations, or drawing on publicly available records (e.g. census data). Many thesis projects, especially in the social sciences, collect data using a survey, in which a **questionnaire** (or "survey instrument") is used to gather information from respondents either online, by mail, face to face, on the telephone, or via videoconference.

Here are a few things to consider when **designing your questionnaire**:

- **Be clear about what you want to measure.** Are you interested in other people's knowledge, attitudes, skills, perceptions, or behaviors? Think about the concepts or variables that are part of your conceptual framework (see Chapter 7), and how you could operationalize them. "Operationalizing" means that you define exactly how you will observe and measure an abstract concept. For example, you might want to measure the concept of "perceived stress." You could do so by asking respondents about how often, over a certain period of time, they felt stressed, were unable to control things in their life, or felt overwhelmed by the number of issues they had to deal with.

- **Strive for clarity.** Keep the questions short, specific, and easy to understand; avoid leading questions and jargon; and ask about only one thing at a time.[4]
- **Use multi-item scales for measuring abstract concepts.** To gain more reliable and accurate results, professional researchers tend to prefer asking multiple, related questions (or "items") about a topic—and not just one question. They call a collection of questions that are intended to measure the same construct a "multi-item scale."[5] (The word "scale" is actually used in two different meanings in research: (a) to describe a set of related "items," and (b) to describe the rating possibilities that survey participants have for responding to a certain item—see Figure 10.1.) For example, to find out about participants' perceived stress levels, we could ask one question with a simple "Yes" or "No" answer: "Have you felt stressed during the past week?" But it would be better to ask three related questions about their stress levels, as in Figure 10.1, each answered with the same scale. The degree of reliability (or internal consistency) of a multi-item scale can be measured with a coefficient called Cronbach's alpha. It describes how closely related the answers are to different questions in one particular scale. For example, if participants generally choose closely related answers to the three questions in Figure 10.1 (e.g. picking only 3s and 4s, or only 0s and 1s), this would indicate the scale is reliable.
- **If possible, use tried-and-tested scales.** A great way of identifying the right survey questions for your own research is to check out which multi-item scales other researchers have used for studying the concepts and variables you have included in your own conceptual framework. For example, you will find different "ready-made" scales for measuring perceived stress, such as the widely used 10-item Perceived Stress Scale (PSS), which was developed by Cohen et al. in 1983.[6] It can save you the time and hassle of creating and testing your own scale if you can find an established scale that has already been tested for reliability. This also makes it easier to compare your results with prior studies.
- **Select an adequate rating scale.** Many questionnaires are based on Likert-type rating scales, in which respondents choose one out of typically five or seven ranked answers (see Table 10.1 for examples). Likert-type scales are easy to understand, but they also have some disadvantages. For example, participants have different response styles (e.g. some people try to avoid extreme answers more than others—this is called the "central tendency bias," which could be overcome at least partially by using an even number of possible answers). Another issue is that, strictly speaking, Likert-type scales produce ordinal data. As the "distance" between the answer options (e.g. between "Never" and "Rarely" versus "Rarely" and "Sometimes") is not necessarily "exactly the

same," it is not totally correct to treat it as an interval scale and calculate, for example, a mean or a standard deviation. Likert-type scales are still often used in this way, but it might make sense to note such measurement issues as potential limitations of your research in the *Discussion* part of your paper.

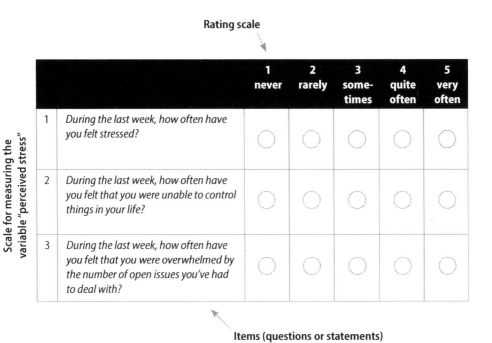

Figure 10.1 Example of a 3-item scale to operationalize the concept of "perceived stress"

What is measured	1	2	3	4	5
Level of agreement	Strongly disagree	Disagree	Neither agree nor disagree	Agree	Strongly agree
Frequency	Never	Rarely	Sometimes	Quite often	Always
Importance	Very low level of importance	Rather low level of importance	Neutral	Rather high level of importance	Very high level of importance
Quality	Very poor	Below average	Average	Above average	Excellent
Likelihood	Definitely not	Probably not	Unsure	Probably yes	Definitely

Table 10.1 Examples of Likert-type scales

At the start of the questionnaire, don't forget to include a short **introductory statement** that informs the survey participants about the purpose of the research.

At the start or end of the survey, you will usually want to collect **demographic data** about the survey participants. Think about what data would be useful for your later statistical analyses. If you are researching an organization, for example, it could be useful to collect demographic data about participants' job roles and seniority, in addition to basic demographic data like age or gender.[7] This could later help you to statistically compare, for example, the results for different departments or levels of hierarchy.

One thing to keep in mind when you conduct survey research is that you will have to rely on the participants answering questions truthfully, which is always a potential source of bias. One way to mitigate this, if your research design allows it, is to also use observations of actual behavior, which could be a more reliable source of data. Otherwise, consider discussing the risk of potential bias when you describe the limitations of your study in the *Discussion* chapter of your thesis (see Chapter 11).

····· **Tip!** ···

There are a few more things to consider when you are planning to develop your own reliable scales for your thesis project, especially when it comes to testing the scales, first through expert validation and then with interview pre-tests and the use of more sophisticated statistical methods such as factor analysis. We recommend you consult articles or book chapters about questionnaire or survey instrument design if you're interested in digging a little deeper into this topic. One good starting point is Mark A. Robinson's article "Using multi-item psychometric scales for research and practice in human resource management."[8]

Choose the right data analysis method

There are two broad ways of analyzing the quantitative data that you have collected: descriptive statistics (in which, as the name suggests, you describe the characteristics of your data) and inferential statistics (where your goal is to make inferences or "predictions" about the population as a whole from your sample).

 **Tip!**

Make sure you "clean" your data first before you start with the data analysis. Data cleaning (or data cleansing) is about removing errors and inconsistencies from the raw data. It includes, for example, correcting misspellings, identifying redundancies or duplicates, excluding cases where important data is missing from the analysis, or consolidating codes (e.g. where gender may have been coded as "f," "F," or "female").

There is a range of quite simple statistical methods that you can use in **descriptive statistics**:

- **Measures of central tendency** such as the *mean* (the mathematical average), the *median* (the central number when all numbers are arranged from the smallest to the largest) or the *mode* (the number that occurs most frequently).
- A first overview of **how the data is distributed** by reviewing the *minimum* (lowest number) and *maximum* (highest number) value of the dataset, as well as the *quartiles* (three data points that divide the dataset into four parts, each presenting 25 percent of the overall set of data points).
- Further **measures of variability or dispersion** are the *range* (the difference between the highest and lowest value), the *variance* (the degree of spread of the data measured as the average squared deviations from the mean), *standard deviation* (the square root of the variance), or *skewness* (a measure of the asymmetry of a distribution).

Which method you choose for **inferential statistics** depends a lot on what you would actually like to find out, but also on the nature of your data. Table 10.2 provides a brief overview of commonly used statistical methods to help you choose the right one for your particular research purpose.

Method	What you can use it for	Example of a research question for which the method could be applied
Chi-square test	Testing hypotheses about whether there is a statistically significant association between two categorical variables.	*Is there an association between school types (public/private) and students entering higher education (higher education/no higher education)?*
Mann–Whitney U test	Testing hypotheses about whether there is a statistically significant difference between two groups (comparing either ordinal or continuous variables, which do not necessarily need to be normally distributed).	*Do students in public and private schools differ in their attitudes toward learning (measured on an ordinal scale)?* *Do learning outcomes (measured on a continuous scale) differ between students in public and private schools?* (This assumes that the data within the groups is skewed/not normally distributed.)
t-test	Testing hypotheses about whether there is a statistically significant difference between two groups (comparing the means of a continuous dependent variable assuming a normal distribution of data).	*Do students in public schools differ from students in private schools in the amount of time spent learning per week?*
One-way ANOVA (Analysis of Variance)	Testing hypotheses about whether there is a statistically significant difference between the means of two or more groups of an independent variable (comparing the means of a normally distributed continuous variable).	*Do students in the first, second, and third grades differ in the amount of time spent learning per week?* (This assumes normal distribution and homogeneity of variance in the data.)
Kruskal–Wallis test	This is the non-parametric alternative to one-way ANOVA (non-parametric means that it is not necessary that the data is normally distributed within the groups). It also allows you to test hypotheses about whether there is a statistically significant difference between the means of more than two groups (comparing the means of a continuous variable).	*Do students in the first, second, and third grades differ in the amount of time spent learning per week?* (This assumes the data within the groups is not normally distributed.)

Method	What you can use it for	Example of a research question for which the method could be applied
Correlation (measured e.g. with Pearson's correlation coefficient or Spearman's rho)	Correlation is a statistical measure that indicates how two (or more) variables change in coordination with each other (i.e. if one is changing, the other(s) are changing too). Pearson's correlation coefficient measures whether there is a linear relationship and indicates the strength of that relationship between two metric variables. Spearman's rho only indicates whether there is a correlation between the variables (no matter if linear or not—it could also be quadratic, for example) and the strength of that relationship. Note that a correlation between variables does not necessarily mean there is a cause-and-effect relationship between them.	*Is there a correlation between the age of students and hours spent learning per week?*
Simple linear regression	Examining whether an independent variable is a good "predictor" of a dependent variable (with an attempt to fit a linear equation to the two variables).	*How much of the variance in learning outcomes (measured in average grades) can be explained by the variance in hours that students spend learning per week?*
Multiple regression	Identifying the extent to which multiple independent variables together explain the variance in the outcome of a dependent variable (measured with the coefficient R-squared or R^2—an R^2 of 0.5 would, for example, mean that half of the observed variation in the dependent variable can be statistically explained by the independent variables).	*How much of the variance in learning outcomes (measured in average grades) can be explained by the combination of the students' ages, the income level of the students' parents, and hours spent learning per week, and how much does each of those factors contribute to the variance in learning outcomes?*

Method	What you can use it for	Example of a research question for which the method could be applied
Hierarchical multiple regression	A form of multiple regression, where independent variables are entered into the statistical model in "blocks" (one after the other), which allows you to check whether newly added independent variables significantly change how much of the variance of the dependent variables can be explained, beyond the effect of the independent variables that had already been entered (i.e. how much R^2 increases when a new independent variable is entered into the statistical model). This also works in the other direction. You can enter all variables first and then remove the non-significant ones step by step.	*How much of the additional variance in learning outcomes (measured in average grades) can be explained by the variance in hours that students spend learning per week, given that differences in age and their parents' income levels have already been considered?*
Factor analysis	Investigating whether there are multiple variables with a similar response pattern and compressing them into a smaller number of factors (that could be unobserved or "latent" variables).	You would like to measure whether certain factors (e.g. the quality of sleep or the amount of physical exercise of a student) influence learning outcomes. You assume that multiple items measure the same latent variable (e.g. *"How often do you sleep less than 6 hours a night?" "How often do you go to bed after midnight?" "How often do you indulge in a marathon series on Netflix at night?" "How often do you go to the bathroom at night?" "How long does it take you to fall asleep?"* for quality of sleep; another five items for physical exercise). Factor analysis will help you statistically determine whether and how you can reduce a larger number of variables (all the items) into a smaller number of factors (in this case the two factors *quality of sleep* and *the amount of physical exercise a student takes*). You then take a look at the extent to which the quality of sleep and/or the amount of physical exercise influences the learning outcomes.

Table 10.2 Commonly used methods in inferential statistics[9]

Once you have identified which analysis method would probably be the most suitable one for your research purpose, turn to research handbooks, articles, or YouTube videos to learn how to apply the method in practice with a statistics software package such as IBM SPSS, or R.

 **Tip!**

In many published quantitative empirical studies, you will come across correlation tables (see Table 10.3 for an example). They are a highly useful tool for providing a quick overview of how different variables are associated with each other. The larger the number, the stronger the relationship between the two variables: +1 indicates a very strong positive relationship, −1 a very strong negative relationship, 0 means that the variables are not related to each other. Asterisks indicate if the relationship between the variables is statistically significant. * indicates a statistically significant correlation at a 0.05 level, ** at a 0.01 level. Using a correlation table for your own data can be a great way to start spotting some interesting relationships between the data. Most thesis advisors would be very happy to see such a table included in the *Results* chapter of your thesis.

	Learning hours	Sleep hours	Exercise hours	Parents' income level	Learning outcome
Learning hours	1				
Sleep hours	−.388**	1			
Exercise hours	.079	−0.204*	1		
Parents' income level	.038	0.087	0.063	1	
Learning outcome	0.407**	−0.497	0.199*	0.214*	1

  * Correlation is significant at a 0.05 level (two-tailed)
  ** Correlation is significant at a 0.01 level (two-tailed)

Table 10.3 An example of a correlation table

How to present your quantitative data in tables and charts

Tables and charts are a great way to present relevant data in the *Results* part of your thesis. The important word here is *relevant*. Make sure you only include data that is **necessary for answering your research question,** and present it in a way that makes it easy for the reader to spot the relevant patterns and relationships in the data.

That's what good tables and charts are all about—rather than just showing "the data," they help the reader to see and grasp **patterns, trends, and the relationship between variables** at a glance.

Here are a few general **tips on using tables and charts** in your thesis:[10]

- Don't overload your thesis with tables and charts. Try to **include some variety** instead. It can be tiring for a reader if you use 10 bar charts or pie charts one after the other.
- **Number tables and charts separately and consecutively** in the order in which they appear in the text (i.e. Table 1, 2, 3, and Figure 1, 2, 3).
- Include a **reference** for all tables and charts in the text (e.g. "As Figure 1 illustrates ..." or "Figure 2 shows that ...").
- Make sure that every table or chart is **self-explanatory**: the reader should be able to understand its meaning without having to read the accompanying text.
- Strive for **simplicity and clarity**: try to focus on communicating one clear message per table or chart instead of cramming as much data as possible into them.
- **Avoid duplicating** the same information in both tables and charts.
- Don't forget to **quote the source** for each table or chart based on someone else's data (if you have changed the original a bit, use "Source: adapted from ...").
- For graphs, make sure to always to **label the axes** and include the **measurement unit** and **scale**.

The most frequently used **types of charts** can be found in Table 10.4. Try to select and apply the one that is most appropriate for the specific data you are trying to present.

Type of chart	What it looks like	What to use it for	What else to consider
Pie chart		Showing relative proportions of a whole (in total the segments should add up to 100%)	• Limit the number of segments to a maximum of 7 (use "other" for the remaining segments) • Include both a label and the percentage for each slice • Don't use a pie chart for other purposes than representing parts of a whole (e.g. for percentages that don't add up to 100%)
Bar chart		Making a comparison between values in different categories (e.g. by gender or age group)	• Don't use misleading scales (ideally, all bars start at a baseline with the value zero) • Organize the bars in a logical order (e.g. from longest to shortest; except when the categories themselves should be ordered in a specific way) • Use horizontal bar charts (with the categories on the vertical axis) when there are many categories
Line chart		Describing changes in a dependent variable over time (to show trends and developments); multi-line charts are also used to show how different groups develop over time compared to each other	• Avoid including too many lines (3–4 lines are usually enough, otherwise the chart can become confusing) • Use equal intervals between the data points (e.g. 2024, 2025, 2026 instead of 2024, 2025, 2030) • Choosing a baseline with the value zero is not always the most effective way to present the data
Histogram		Describing the frequency distribution of a numeric variable	• Use it only for numerical data (for categorical data, use a bar chart) • Use a baseline with the value zero • Don't leave gaps between the bars of the histogram (which are called "bins")
XY scatter plot		Showing the relationship (especially correlation) between two variables	• Be careful not to indicate cause-and-effect relationships when a third variable that is not part of the scatter plot is the cause of the variation of both variables (don't mistake correlation for causation) • Think about whether adding a trend line could help illustrate the direction of the relationship between the variables

Table 10.4 An overview of frequently used types of charts

Tip!

You may want to copy tables or figures from other sources to use in your thesis. Remember that if these tables or figures are copyrighted material, you'll need to seek permission from the rightsholder first to reproduce them—simply adding a citation might not be enough.

Whenever you use a table or chart, remember that they have one main purpose to fulfill—**to make it easier for the reader to understand and interpret the relevant data,** and not to confuse the reader by presenting *all* the data that you have collected or analyzed in your empirical work.

Tip!

Don't just unthinkingly copy and paste screenshots or tables from statistical analysis software packages (like SPSS or R) into your thesis. They usually show much more data than is really relevant. Books about how to use software packages for statistical analysis (e.g. Andy Field's books about SPSS or R)[11] provide useful advice about which data is really relevant to report on for specific statistical analysis methods.

Ensuring the quality of your quantitative research

Many thesis advisors or dissertation committees will want you to show that your empirical work conforms with **three main quality criteria** for quantitative research:

1. **Objectivity**—the degree to which the research results remain unaffected by who the researcher is and what their feelings or opinions are.
2. **Reliability**—the extent to which results can be consistently replicated when the same research instrument or research process is used again (but beware: if something is reliable, it does not necessarily mean that it's accurate!).
3. **Validity**—the degree to which a research instrument really measures what was intended to be measured (here's where accuracy comes in).

To make things more complex, there are actually **different types of validity**. Here are some types that you will often come across in research:

- **External validity**—whether the results that were found are generalizable, i.e. whether what was measured in an experiment or sample really reflects what we wanted to measure in the "real world" or a population as a whole.
- **Internal validity**—the degree to which we can confidently conclude that changes in a dependent variable are really attributable to changes in the independent variable, and not to some other factors that explain the link.
- **Construct validity**—the extent to which the measurement tool (e.g. a scale) adequately represents the abstract construct (or concept) that it is supposed to measure.

Carefully consider the quality criteria *before* you conduct your research—afterwards it's usually too late.

Table 10.5 gives a brief overview of some methods that you could use to ensure objectivity, reliability, and validity. Take it as a starting point for checking out the methods further, as including details about all of them would go well beyond the scope of this book.

Quality criterion	Methods for ensuring it
Objectivity	• Avoid holding predetermined ideas about the outcome of the study. • Make sure the research participants are not influenced in any way by you as a researcher. • Document your methodological decisions (including reasons for choosing certain data collection and data analysis methods).
Reliability	• Use the test-retest method (using the same instrument twice with the same group of respondents). • Use the interrater method (let different researchers conduct the same measurement or observe the same subjects—and then use statistical methods like Cohen's Kappa to measure the level of congruence between the different "raters"). • Use Cronbach's alpha to measure the internal consistency of different items in a scale (see the section on designing a questionnaire earlier in this chapter).
External validity	• Make sure you use an appropriate sampling method (random sampling can be particularly useful for improving external validity; see the section on sampling at the beginning of this chapter). • Use a large sample. • Ensure low drop-out rates from your selected sample (e.g. through contacting potential respondents several times). • Describe in detail how the participants in the sample were recruited from the overall target population. • Try to get a heterogeneous and diverse sample (e.g. including respondents from different places or various age groups).

Quality criterion	Methods for ensuring it
Internal validity	• Use randomized controlled trials (assigning participants to treatment and control groups on a random basis—this is often used in medical research). • Include control variables in your research design (other variables that could have an impact on the dependent variables), and then use statistical control methods.
Construct validity	• Explain in detail the steps that you are taking to operationalize the broader concepts that you intend to measure in your study. • Use confirmatory factor analysis as a statistical method for evaluating construct validity.

Table 10.5 Selected methods for ensuring objectivity, reliability, and validity in a quantitative empirical study

Before you start worrying too much about meeting quality criteria, let's acknowledge that some of the quality assurance methods in Table 10.5 will be difficult to implement for a limited-scale thesis project. But maybe there are one or two that you would still want to consider applying in your thesis. Using some of these methods and then describing how you used them in your *Method* section will certainly put a benevolent smile on your advisor's face.

 **Thesis writing summary #10** ·····································

- **Choose an appropriate sampling method.** The way in which you select your study participants from a larger group (the "population") has a strong effect on whether your research results will be generalizable or not. Probability sampling methods are preferable in terms of ensuring representativeness.
- **Invest enough time and effort to create a good questionnaire.** If your main data collection method is using a survey, this will be one of the best investments you will make during your thesis project. Try to use multiple-item scales instead of just individual questions when you intend to measure abstract concepts.
- **Choose the right data analysis method.** Find out which method best suits your research purpose, then consult specialized literature on quantitative methods to learn how to analyze and interpret your data with the help of statistical analysis software.
- **Use tables and charts to present data that is relevant for answering your research question.** Create them in a way that makes it easy for the reader to spot patterns, trends, and relationships between variables "at first sight."
- **Consider the quality criteria for quantitative research.** Include some sentences in the *Method* section of your thesis about how you have ensured the objectivity, reliability, and validity of your research.

How to present and discuss your findings

Let's start with some good news: if you've completed all the steps that we've discussed in the previous chapters, you're getting close to the finishing line.

In this chapter, we will focus on the **final three chapters** that you will need to complete for your thesis:

1. The *Results* chapter, where you present the findings of your empirical research in a structured way.
2. The *Discussion* chapter, where you interpret the findings and connect them to the existing literature.
3. The *Conclusion* chapter, in which you provide an answer to your main research question along with some concluding statements and recommendations for practice.

Let's take a closer look at what advisors and examination committees typically expect you to present in each of those chapters.

Results

The purpose of the *Results* chapter is to **report your study's main findings**. Your job here is to communicate the essence of what you found in your data related to your research questions. Do not interpret the results or compare them with the existing literature (that will be part of the *Discussion* chapter), but purely describe your key findings—and try to do so in an unbiased and objective way.

"Key" findings means that the *Results* chapter shouldn't become a "data dump." It's not about cramming all the data that you have into this chapter. Focus instead on reporting what is really important for answering your research question.

 **Tip!**

Make sure that you present your findings in a logically structured way. Ideally, your *Results* chapter should read like a convincing and coherent story. One way to achieve this is to first create an outline of the chapter. Think about the structure you would like to use to present your data, decide on the main headings for the sections and subsections, and put your thoughts into a logical sequence before you start writing. There's more on planning your writing in Chapter 12.

The *Results* chapter will typically start with a short introduction in which you restate the purpose of your study and describe how the chapter is organized. The remainder of the chapter will look different depending on the research methodology that you used.

For a **qualitative study**:

- **Organize your findings in a logical way.** You could, for example, use research questions, key themes or topics that emerged from your data, or the main concepts from your conceptual framework as an organizing principle. Alternatively, a chronological order might make sense if it's important for answering your research question to understand how events unfolded over time. Use headings and subheadings to make your structure visible to the reader.
- **Present your results in a narrative form.** Be a good storyteller, aiming to both vividly and accurately present all the relevant facts in a way that is easy to understand and engaging for the reader.
- **Reveal patterns in the data.** Focus on common themes and try to condense and "simplify" larger amounts of data. Provide general observations about what the data shows. Focus on the recurring themes—the trends and patterns, or similarities and differences between different groups—rather than just listing raw data.
- **Include verbatim quotes.** Use them to provide evidence. Rich details from your interviews or observations add to the credibility of your research. Remember to quote in moderation: too many very long quotes may bore the reader.
- **Don't restrict yourself to reporting results that support your assumptions.** Remember to stay objective and try to include everything that's relevant, including data that might be inconsistent or that contradicts your anticipations.

- **Make use of visual displays.** Include tables and figures in the *Results* chapter. The old saying that "a picture is worth a thousand words" is particularly true for this part of your thesis. Think about how you could visualize the data, for example in matrices which show patterns at a glance, or in diagrams which neatly present the essence of your findings (see Chapter 10 for examples).

If some of the analysis tables or other visual displays become very extensive, or if they would interfere with the flow of the text, consider putting them into an appendix at the end of your thesis.

Tip!

Create figures and tables first, then write your narrative as a "commentary" around these visual displays. This will help to give structure to your writing, and it can also make the writing task easier, as the data displays already give you a clear outline of what to focus on in your narrative.[1]

For a **quantitative study**, the *Results* chapter typically includes the following information:

- **Demographic data about your sample.** If your sample consists of people, you could, for example, report on age, gender distribution, or nationality. If the sample consists of companies, demographic data might include company size, location, or industry (whatever is relevant for assessing the representativeness of your sample).
- **The reliability of your data.** When you are using scales in which several items (or questions) are combined to measure one construct, you need to report on the reliability of these scales. One measure that is often used for that purpose is Cronbach's alpha, which tells you whether the items are "internally consistent" (closely related to each other). A widely used rule of thumb is that Cronbach's alpha values should be higher than 0.7 for a scale to be acceptable. Another issue that needs to be considered and reported on in most quantitative studies is the "shape" of your data (whether it is normally distributed or not), because of the impact that it has on which statistical analysis methods you are "allowed" to use.
- **Descriptive statistics.** In this section, you will typically report on frequency statistics, central tendencies (e.g. the mean) and spread (e.g. the standard devi-

ation) of your relevant data. Some students do not go beyond descriptive statistics in their analysis, which is a pity, because the really interesting results are usually only found with further analysis like correlation, inferential statistics, and hypothesis tests. Don't skip these—your advisor and examination committee will highly value their inclusion.

- **Correlation analysis.** There are different statistical methods of calculating the degree to which your variables are moving in the same direction, for example Pearson's or Spearman's correlation analysis. You will usually summarize the results of a correlation analysis (including measures for the strength and significance of the correlation of your variables) in a correlation table.
- **Inferential statistics and hypothesis tests.** Inferential statistics help you draw conclusions and make generalizations from your sample about the population that it represents. There are a range of different statistical tests that you can use for testing your hypotheses, including *comparison tests* that help you assess similarities and differences between different groups (such as the t-test, ANOVA, or the Mann–Whitney U test) and *regression analysis* (e.g. linear, multiple linear, logistic, nominal, or ordinal regression), which can be used to estimate the relationship between variables (see also Chapter 10).

In whatever way you want to present your data, be sure to end the *Results* chapter with a short summary paragraph in which you **succinctly recap your key findings**.

Discussion

After presenting your findings in the *Results* chapter, it's now time to **interpret** them in the *Discussion* chapter. Do not include any new findings here, but reflect on your research results, explain what they mean, relate them to prior literature, and discuss their theoretical and practical implications.

Here are the main questions that you should answer in the *Discussion* part of your thesis:

1. **What are the most important results and insights from your analysis?** You will typically summarize these insights in one or two paragraphs at the beginning of your *Discussion* chapter—but make sure you don't just reiterate what you have already written in the *Results* chapter.
2. **How are these results related to previous research?** Describe where your findings confirm results from prior studies, and where they differ. Provide plausible reasons and explanations for the results. Mention specific prior studies here (e.g. "There is a contradiction with what McGregor (2022) observed …") rather than just general statements such as "This contradicts the existing literature …"

3. **Are there different ways of interpreting the results?** Acknowledge that there might be different perspectives on what your findings could mean. Most advisors and examination committees value critical thinking and an approach in which you challenge your own assumptions and offer alternative interpretations.

4. **What is the theoretical contribution of your work?** Explain how the findings of your study add to the existing knowledge in the field. For example, are you providing a new perspective on relationships between different constructs or variables, or a new explanation for such relationships, or have you shown that a certain model or theory is applicable in a specific domain that has not been the focus of research before? Inform the reader how your research helps them to better understand a phenomenon.

5. **What are the limitations of your research?** No study is perfect—not even highly experienced researchers would dare to claim that they are. That's why you should always include a few sentences about your study's methodological limitations. You could, for example, highlight issues with the sampling procedure, a small sample size, the non-representativeness of the sample (and therefore limits to the generalizability of the results), limited access to relevant data, potential biases in the data collection process (e.g. self-reporting bias), variables that are potentially not independent of one another, measures with low reliability levels (e.g. with a Cronbach's alpha below 0.7), or cultural bias, to name just a few.

6. **What are your ideas for further research?** The limitations of your study can be a good starting point for discussing how they could potentially be overcome by further research. It is generally good practice to include some ideas of how further studies could build on your findings and extend the knowledge in the domain that you are studying (this section is sometimes also called "Outlook").

Some research papers also include **implications for practice** in the *Discussion* chapter. Alternatively, you can make your recommendations for practice in the *Conclusion* chapter.

Conclusion

The *Conclusion* chapter (sometimes also called *Conclusions and Recommendations*) is usually a very short one. It contains—unsurprisingly—your conclusions, as well as recommendations for practice.

Your **conclusions** should always be based on synthesizing and integrating the results of both your literature review and empirical work. You should not come up with any new data or "surprising" new results at this stage, nor should your conclusions represent your personal opinion. Instead of asserting *"To conclude, it's better to play basketball than football, because basketball has a lower risk of injury"* (*"it's better"* is an opinion), write *"In line with prior research, the results of this study confirm that basketball has a considerably lower risk of injury than football. This means that the risk of injury in physical education classes could be reduced with a higher share of basketball in preference to football"* (this is a logical conclusion).

Be careful not to equate "conclusions" with "findings" and simply reiterate your findings as a result. While your findings are "the facts," your conclusions are the results of your analysis and your **interpretations** of the findings.[2] You should go beyond "what I found out" to "what does it mean" here. Provide "takeaway messages" for the reader that clearly state "what you now know, having done this research, that you did not know before."[3]

One of the main purposes of the *Conclusion* is to **answer your main research question**. Restate it once again, and try to provide a clear and concise answer.

One thing to avoid in the *Conclusion* (and elsewhere) are grandiose statements like *"This study clearly proves that ..."* (there's hardly any single study that proves something beyond doubt) or *"This is a really important contribution ..."* (let the reader decide on this).[4] Try to stay humble and let your research speak for itself.

The other main element of the *Conclusion* chapter is your **recommendations**. Think about the implications of your research for practice. Explain what your research results could mean for practitioners, and how people "in the real world" will be able to profit from your findings.

You could, for example, show how implementing your findings could help people to improve their professional practice, or how your findings could become the basis for new policies that could contribute to solving a particular problem.

So the *Conclusion* chapter summarizes the insights and new learnings that you and others could gain from your research work. As the name of the chapter neatly indicates, it also concludes the main part of your thesis.

After that, you will just have to include a complete **list of references** (in alphabetical order and in the correct referencing format—see Chapter 15) and maybe add some **appendices** which include your interview guide or questionnaire for your survey, interview transcripts, coding guidelines, coding tables, or other ancillary material. Then you'll have made it to the end—all the parts of your thesis will be there!

Thesis writing summary #11 ·······················

- **Report key results in the *Results* chapter.** Objectively present the results of your data analysis in a logically structured way, but do not interpret the data yet. Apply the right format for this chapter based on your research method (the structure will be different for qualitative and quantitative research), and use the power of visual displays like tables and figures.
- **Interpret the results in the *Discussion* chapter.** Summarize the most important findings, relate them to previous research, provide interpretations, highlight the contributions of your research, acknowledge the limitations, and suggest some ideas for further research.
- **Provide compelling conclusions in the *Conclusion* chapter.** Succinctly summarize what we can learn from your research, provide a clear answer to your main research question, and include some recommendations for changes in policy or practice based on your research findings.

PART III

Writing your thesis

Surviving your thesis project is so much easier if you can write with confidence.

In this part, you will learn:

how to plan and start writing,
how to write like an academic,
how to build up an argument,
how to use references and avoid plagiarism,
how to fix grammar, punctuation, and spelling issues,
and how to edit and finish off your thesis.

How to plan and start writing

Do you struggle with writing? You're not alone if so: most people do, even the ones who enjoy it. In the next few chapters we'll give lots of tips on how to improve the style, structure, and clarity of your writing so it's more likely to impress your readers. In this chapter we'll give some advice on **how to get *started* writing**, which can often seem like the hardest hurdle to overcome.

Something that can help immensely is having a detailed plan from which to write. This gives you a solid starting point, and helps to make the whole writing process smoother and easier. It means you're much more likely to end up with a well-structured thesis. You'll also find writing your thesis less stressful if you plan your schedule carefully, so you know you've got enough time to write each section.

So let's start with planning.

Planning your time

Writing a thesis will definitely be a calmer experience if you're not rushing to get it all done just before the deadline. You'll also produce higher-quality work if you leave enough time to plan carefully, really think through your arguments, and then write (and rewrite) and edit your work. So, early on, **work out how much time you need and make sure you set this time aside**.

It might seem impossible to work out how much time you need to write a whole thesis, but the answer here is to break it down into smaller chunks. Chapter 2 explains how to do this, but here's a brief reminder:

- Work out roughly how many words you need to write for each chapter.
- Work out roughly how many words you can write in an hour (or a day).
- From this, work out how many hours (or days) you need to write each chapter.
- Block out that time in your calendar (make sure this is realistic: leave room for other commitments and breaks, and add in some contingency time too).
- Don't forget to leave some time at the end for editing and proofreading (see Chapter 17).

As we said in Chapter 2, you don't want to wait until you find time for writing your thesis, because that might never happen—you need to proactively make time by blocking it out in your calendar before it fills up with other things. And to do that accurately, you first need to work out how much time you need.

Planning your writing

You might feel that planning is a waste of time that could be more usefully spent on other things (like actually writing), but it's worth doing. It gives you confidence that you've got something to say. It makes writing your thesis quicker and less overwhelming because you've taken away the burden of working out what to write next: you simply have to follow your plan and write it. It also makes for a better-structured thesis, which will get you more marks.

A plan is like a map you can follow as you write. It doesn't have to be fixed—you can change it as you discover new information or develop your arguments. Below we've described the steps you can take to create a detailed plan, where you end up with a rough idea of what you're going to write in each paragraph, with all of the information you need to flesh out those paragraphs in one document.

But planning is personal, so do adapt this approach to suit you. For example, if you're a visual thinker then you may want to use mind maps to help pin down the structure or content of a chapter. In the course of your studies you may have already settled on a good way to plan your essays, in which case stick with what works for you and do the same for your thesis (though you may still want to tweak your plan using some of the advice below).

1. Make a high-level list

Pick a chapter of your thesis, and **make a brief list of the most important things it needs to do** (Part II of this book will help you here). Table 12.1 provides a few examples.

Literature Review (see Chapter 6)	Method (see Chapter 8)	Discussion (see Chapter 11)
• Summarize the most relevant existing research, in a structured way • Critically evaluate this research	• Describe my method—in enough detail for someone else to replicate it	• Explain research results • Relate them to prior literature • Discuss theoretical (and practical?) implications

Table 12.1 An example of a high-level list for planning your writing

2. Expand the list

Take your high-level list and break it down further, so you've written down the main points your chapter needs to cover. (Again, you can use Part II of this book to help you work out what to include.) You can find examples in Table 12.2 for the *Method* and *Discussion* chapters. You don't need to worry too much at this stage about getting things in the right order; you just want to make sure you've covered everything important.

Method	Discussion
• The research question and purpose of the research • Summary of the method used • Why this method was chosen • The sampling procedure and population/sample size • Instructions used to collect the data • Method of collecting the data • Method of analyzing the data • Ethical considerations • Ensuring research quality	• Summary of the most important results and insights • How the results relate to previous research • Different ways of interpreting the results • Theoretical contribution of work to the field • Limitations of the research • Ideas for further research

Table 12.2 An example of an expanded list for planning your writing of the *Method* and *Discussion* chapters

3. Paste in your notes

Use the bullet points from your list as headings. Add them to a document, then below each heading paste in any relevant information, quotations, ideas and thoughts from all of the notes you've made during the course of your reading and research. Essentially, you're trying to **distill all of your notes into one document for each chapter**; they'll be jumbled up, but roughly grouped according to your headings.

 **Tip!**

To help prevent plagiarism and make referencing much easier (see Chapter 15), make it clear in your notes when you're directly quoting someone else (e.g. put this text in quotation marks, or a different colored font). For each quotation, add a reference (including a page number). Where you talk about other people's research in your own words, also add a reference.

Consider putting your own ideas, evaluations and arguments in a different color—this can help you make sure you're including critical analysis (see Chapter 14) and your writing is not purely descriptive, which is important for reaching higher marks. See Chapter 4 for more on how to take smart notes.

....

4. Organize your notes

Now start trying to **organize your notes in a logical order**. This is when you'll start to get a sense of what each paragraph (or every two or three paragraphs) is all about.

As you're doing this, try to always consider if the structure you're creating flows well. As we'll discuss in Chapter 14, a good question to keep in mind is "What does the reader need to know or understand for this to make sense?" Then make sure that information comes first.

Under each heading, start to **put the main points in bold**. In Figure 12.1, you'll find a simple example using the first bullet point of the list created in Table 12.2 for the *Discussion* chapter.

Summary of the most important results and insights

Important result 1: charities receive more public donations when they are more specific about where the money is going

[Notes on own research results showing this]

[Notes on other research literature that backs this up]

Insight from important result 1: to take advantage of this, charities need to set up systems that mean money donated to a particular project does actually go to that project

[Notes explaining why this can be difficult, using research literature]

[Notes explaining why this is still worth doing]

Figure 12.1 An example of how to organize your notes

You might notice that the notes in Figure 12.1 cover not just the first bullet point in the *Discussion* list above ("Summary of the most important results and insights"), but also the second bullet point ("How the results relate to previous research"). So you might end up deciding to cover these two bullet points alongside each other, rather than one after the other. It's OK if your plan evolves messily and organically like this. For the *Literature Review*, in particular, it may not be until you start trying to arrange and group your notes together that you work out what your main points are. In effect, organizing your notes (step 4) may lead you to work out your headings (step 2).

But in the end you'll know more or less what you want to write for every paragraph. You'll have most of the notes you need to support what you're going to say pulled together and organized in one document. You'll likely have some gaps and holes, but it'll be easier to see where these are. You can then go away and do more research or reading to fill them in, or highlight them and make a note to fill them in once you start writing (but beware that these holes will slow you down, and you probably won't want to stumble across too many of them as you write).

 **Tip!**

If you are a visual thinker, you might find it helpful to create a visual outline of a chapter (similar to the thesis outline we suggested in Chapter 5) as you organize your notes. Such an outline could, for example, include boxes that represent the main topics you intend to cover in that part of the thesis, connected with arrows that show how these topics are logically linked to each other. You can then use the visual outline as a "map" that will guide you through your writing.

5. Review your plan

You then want to **check your plan**.

- Does it cover all the important stuff? Check back against the lists you created for steps 1 and 2. Is there anything missing?
- Does it flow logically? Is the structure coherent? You can try reverse outlining (see Chapter 17) to check your plan flows well.

If you've followed all the steps above then you should have a really solid plan, which means you've done a lot of the hard work before you even start writing. But what about the writing itself? Let's take a look at that now.

How to start writing

At some point you're going to have to stop researching, reading, planning, and procrastinating, and actually start writing your thesis. If you're struggling to make yourself sit down and start, or you're staring at a blank page and haven't got a clue how to begin, the advice below will hopefully propel you forward. (You might also want to go back and reread the advice in Chapter 1.)

Treat writing like a job

You might feel you have to wait until you feel motivated or inspired to write, but that can mean you never write, because you're never quite in exactly the right mood or zone—completely alert, raring to go, where it feels like the words will fly from your fingertips perfectly formed.

It's much better to treat writing like a job. It's just something that you've got to do. There are no real shortcuts or magic tricks; you've just got to get the words down on the page. Even the best writers often find writing a struggle, but they **make themselves keep writing**.

So don't wait for inspiration or motivation. It doesn't matter if you're feeling tired or reluctant. You can still sit down and make yourself write and the words will come out. They may not be the best words you've ever written, but it's still progress, and it's much easier to come back later and improve them than come back later to nothing at all.

Just make yourself sit down and start writing.

Plan properly

As we said above, if you've got an idea of what you want to say, and an order in which you want to say it, then the writing becomes much easier. If you're really not sure what to write, it may be because you haven't done enough reading or research yet, or enough thinking about what you want to say.

 **Tip!**

All writers are different, and some do find it easier to write without a detailed plan. They write a very rough draft first, doing bits of research as they go along, then sort out the structure and fill in the holes. This can be a helpful way to work out what you already know and where you definitely need to do more research and reading. But if you go with this approach, then bear in mind that at some point you're going to have to make sure your thesis is sensibly structured and flows well. You can't skip this step, and it's generally easier to do when planning.

Start with the easy bits

If you've got a solid plan, then you can **jump around between sections and write the easiest bits first**. Then you can work on joining everything together once you've got a first draft. The progress you make on the easier sections will give you motivation to work on the harder sections.

Try answering questions

If you're stuck staring at a blank page then try using questions as prompts. Take the main points in your plan (see above) and **turn them into questions**. These might be overarching questions that you can then break down into smaller ones, so each paragraph or even every few sentences answers a specific question (e.g. "How does Mierlo's research support my argument?", "Why did I choose this particular sample size?", and "What was the most important result from my research?").

Try writing down these questions and then answering them as directly as possible. You'll obviously want to refine your writing later on, but a first draft just to get you going might look something like this:

What was the most important result from my research?

The most important result from my research is that…

Why is that the most important result?

This finding is important because…

Does this match other people's research?

This matches Cavez's research because she says …

Take tiny steps

We mentioned this in Chapter 1, and it's an approach that works well here too. **Break things down**, so you're not thinking "I've got to write a whole dissertation," or even "I've got to write 1,000 words." Think "I'm going to write for 10 minutes" or "I'm going to write until I've got the first draft of a paragraph on X" or "I'm going to write 100 words."

Lower your expectations (writing = rewriting)

This is perhaps the most important secret of writing: **good writing involves an awful lot of rewriting**. This is especially true for more complex writing like academic writing. Often it's not something you're aware of, because most of the time you only ever see the finished, polished product. But most of the time those sentences you're reading in the novel or the journal article you've got in your hands have not come out of the writer's fingertips perfectly formed. They might have needed many revisions.

Writing by rewriting takes a lot of the pressure off getting started. Effectively, you're lowering your expectations for what you've got to achieve. Instead of sitting down to write a polished paragraph, you're just sitting down to write a rough paragraph where your aim is to simply get your thoughts down in more or less the right order.

Here's how to do it. Start by writing down ideas in note form, rather than nicely formed sentences. These are basically the main points you want to make. Here's an example:

Feeling part of a company is motivating (Maslow's love and belonging needs)

So companies want to create a culture where people belong (like a family)

One way to do this is to allow people to ask questions, speak up, share their thoughts, etc.

Like at Pixar

Then start to fill out those points, again writing in note form. You might want to use a different colored font to signal to yourself that you're writing in notes and it's fine if it's messy; it doesn't have to be perfect. Your main aim is to just get down the points you want to make, without worrying about how they're expressed.

One of Maslow's hierarchy of needs is "love and belonging"—when a company fulfills this need for its employees this motivates them to work harder (e.g. Doolin, 2008; Turner, 1998). So this means that companies want to create a culture where people feel like they belong. This is why companies want to give the impression they're like a "family" that "loves" its employees. One way companies can do this is by encouraging people to ask questions, raise concerns, speak up, etc. So they feel heard. Pixar is one company known for creating this type of culture where people are encouraged to say what they think.

Then rewrite this again, so it's closer to the final version.

One level in Maslow's hierarchy of needs is "love and belonging," which refers to a sense of belonging and acceptance. Studies such as Turner (1998) and Doolin (2008) show that when a company fulfills this need for its employees, they are motivated to work harder. This is one reason why companies often want to create a culture where people feel like they belong, and why they encourage the perception that they are like a "family" that "loves" its employees. One way that companies can create this sense of belonging is by encouraging their employees to make their voices heard, so they feel empowered to contribute, ask questions, and raise concerns. Pixar is one company well known for creating this type of culture where employees are encouraged to contribute openly and honestly.

If you have a very detailed plan where you know exactly what you want to say, you might prefer to more or less polish each paragraph before moving on to the next one. Or you might want to write a whole section or chapter in note form before going back and rewriting it in proper sentences.

Of course this rewriting takes time, and you'll need to allow for that, but it makes the whole process of writing a lot less daunting because you're tackling it in smaller steps rather than trying to jump from blank page to finished thesis in one go.

Remember, you're just trying to be clear

When do you stop rewriting? It's possible to rewrite and rewrite and tweak until you have perfect, sparkling sentences … but that would take too much time and also it isn't what people are expecting from you. Your main aim is just to **get your ideas across clearly, in a style that isn't too informal** (see Chapter 13). If you've turned a paragraph of notes into one of complete sentences, where it's clear what you mean, then job done. Pat yourself on the back and move on to the next paragraph.

Remind yourself that you can do this

If you've got to this point in your studies then you've probably had to write essays before, and they've probably been OK. So think of your thesis as simply being like a bigger essay, or three or four essays combined. You can write this thesis because you've already basically done it before. Sure, it's probably longer than anything you've previously written, but that's just a case of getting more words down on the page. And if you think of your thesis as a series of discrete chapters, then it really is just like writing a series of essays. You've done it before, and you can do it again now.

How to keep writing

Once you've started writing you've got over the biggest hurdle, and the trick becomes finding the motivation to keep writing. Some of the tips above will help with this, as will the advice in Chapter 1. Here are a few more ideas that might help.

Keep writing every day

Or every other day. **Try to keep the momentum going**, even if you only manage to write for 10 minutes or don't write more than a couple of paragraphs. This helps to prevent the act of writing from building itself up into an intimidating mental block that makes it hard to get going again.

Take breaks and give yourself rewards

Writing is hard work, and it requires a lot of mental effort. **Take regular breaks, and promise yourself rewards** for hitting a word count or completing a chapter.

Get early (positive) feedback on your work

Try to find a cheerleader: someone who'll read your work and tell you what's good about it, and motivate you to keep going. See if your advisor, a relative or a friend will give you early feedback on your writing. They could helpfully point out improvements you could make, too, but what you mainly want here is someone to tell you you're doing a good job, and to keep going.

Set yourself accountable deadlines

If you've planned your time carefully (see the start of this chapter), then you'll have probably set yourself a string of little deadlines to hit, such as for finishing each chapter (or even specific sections within each chapter). To make these deadlines harder to ignore, **tell someone else about them**. The simple act of doing this will likely make you take the deadline more seriously, and your "accountability buddy" can then check in with you to make sure you're actually hitting your deadlines.

Thesis writing summary #12

- **Plan your time so you're not rushing to finish your thesis.** Work out how much time you need to write each chapter and make sure you block out this time in your calendar.
- **Create a detailed plan for each chapter before you start writing it.** This gives you a roadmap of what you want to say in more or less every paragraph. While such detailed planning takes time, it makes the writing process much easier and leads to a better-structured thesis.
- **There are various tricks and techniques you can use to help you start writing.** These include writing messy notes to start with (and then turning them into well-written paragraphs); using questions as prompts; and treating writing like a job rather than waiting for inspiration to strike.
- **Once you've started writing, you need to find something that motivates you to keep going.** Try setting accountable deadlines, rewarding yourself for hitting word counts, or finding someone who will act as your cheerleader.

How to write like an academic

From all the reading you've been doing for your studies, you'll have probably noticed that academic writing has its own style. It's quite different to most non-fiction writing you come across on a day-to-day basis, like social media updates, news sites, and magazine articles. It should be formal yet clear, and objective yet persuasive. It can be tricky to find the right balance, and even when you can easily spot an academic style, translating this into your own writing can be hard if you're not used to it.

This chapter covers six principles for writing like an academic. You'll learn how to be formal, clear, concise, cautious, precise, and objective in your writing.

Be formal

One of the things that sets academic writing apart is its formality. We'll go on to see how this does not necessarily mean writing a lot of long, complicated sentences. But it does mean **avoiding the following**:

- **Text speak** like *gr8* (great), *IMHO* (in my humble opinion) and *ppl* (people).
- **Casual, informal words** like *sort of, things, okay, maybe* and *like*.
- **Slang and colloquial expressions.** These are informal words and phrases that aren't understood by everyone. It includes "new" words like *sussy* for "suspicious," as well as regular words used in a context some people might not understand, like *fire* being used as a compliment rather than to describe something hot and burning. It also includes whole phrases where the meaning isn't obvious, like *Let me catch forty winks*, meaning "Let me have a short sleep," or *There's more than one way to skin a cat*, meaning "There's more than one way to get something done." Watch out for all of these and avoid using them in your writing.
- **Contractions.** These are shortened versions of words, which often have an apostrophe in them. For example, *don't* rather than *do not*, *it'll* rather than *it will*, and *they're* rather than *they are*.

- **Abbreviations that are less accepted in academic writing.** Some abbreviations are perfectly fine to use, like *BCE* (Before Common Era), *USD* (US dollars), or *am* (morning). Ones you should generally try to avoid are *e.g.* (use *for example* or *such as*), *i.e.* (use *for instance*), *etc.* (use *and so on*), *NB* (use *note that*), and *vs* (use *versus*).
- **Sentences that are incomplete or grammatically incorrect.** See page 167 in Chapter 14 for more on this.

Table 13.1 gives an example of a paragraph that's too informal rewritten in a more appropriate style.

Too informal	More formal
Lots of voters feel like their vote doesn't count in this country. This is partly thanks to the first-past-the-post system that we've got. But it's hard to change the system when it's so good for those in power.	Many voters in the UK feel as if their vote counts for little in a general election, which is partly a result of the first-past-the-post system. However, it is difficult to transform the voting system when it benefits the ruling party.

Table 13.1 An example of a paragraph rewritten in a more formal style

Academic writing also tends to **avoid using "I"** (*I* analyzed the results, *I* agree with Brown's conclusions, etc.). This makes the writing more objective and formal, and keeps the focus on your research and findings, rather than on you. But it's best to check this with your advisor, as this can vary between universities and disciplines and even the type of writing (for example, a reflective piece of writing might be better using "I").

 **Tip!**

As well as avoiding "I," you also want to avoid "you." Instead of writing phrases like "You will see from these results that," or "You may notice here that Wood refutes Gordon's claims," say instead "These results show that" or "It is noticeable that Wood refutes Gordon's claims."

In Table 13.2, you can find a few examples of how to avoid using "I."

Using "I"	Rewritten version
In this chapter, I will examine my findings …	*This chapter will examine the findings from …*
I tested the samples …	*Samples were tested …*
I am persuaded by Chen's assertion that …	*Chen's assertion is persuasive because …*
I calculated the wind speed and this led me to realize …	*Calculating the wind speed led to the realization that …*
I needed to conduct more experiments so I could be sure of my results …	*More experiments were conducted to verify the results …*

Table 13.2 Examples of how to avoid using "I"

Be clear

It can be easy to assume that to be respected as an academic you have to use long words and complicated sentences, but this isn't true. One study of academic writing actually found that more complex writing can make you sound *less* intelligent.[1] Writing clearly makes your ideas and arguments easier to understand, your thesis much more enjoyable to read, and whoever marks it more likely to take notice of what you've got to say.

Here are some tips on writing clearly.

Make sure your point is clear

Your advisor isn't a mind reader, and you don't want them to sit scratching their head trying to work out what you mean. So what are you really trying to say? Put the point you want to make in the simplest, clearest way you can. Start by just saying it out loud or writing it down without worrying about trying to sound academic. You could begin your thought with the phrase "What I really mean is …"[2] Then once your point is crystal clear, you can write it out more formally. Table 13.3 provides an example.

What I really mean is ...	More academic version
Benson's evidence isn't strong enough.	*Because of its small sample size and lack of randomization, Benson's study by itself cannot support this hypothesis.*
Countries need to export goods.	*Exporting is seen as vital to the economic development of many countries.*

Table 13.3 Examples of converting a clear point into an academic writing style

Create a logical, coherent structure

Making sure your point is clear isn't just important when writing individual sentences—it also matters as you build those sentences into paragraphs and those paragraphs into whole sections of text. You can use "What I really mean is ..." at all these different levels, for example to help you work out the main point of a paragraph or a section. Summarize the paragraph or section in one sentence starting "What I really mean is ...", and then check what you've written does actually reflect that summary.

Ideas should flow logically and coherently to build up a well-structured overall argument that is easy to understand. See Chapter 14 for more on this.

Embrace shorter sentences

Sometimes academic writing requires longer sentences to express complex thoughts, and that's fine, but try to keep sentences shorter where possible. (Though remember that your sentences still need to be whole and grammatically correct; you don't want to slip into writing notes.)

Reread any longer sentences that you've written. Once you get to the end of the sentence, can you remember the start? Do you understand what the sentence means as a whole? Can you hold the whole sentence in your head? If not, see if you can break it down. Look for where the commas are in the sentence, or connecting words like "and" or "but," and see if you can split the sentence there.

In Table 13.4, you can find an example of one long sentence split into three shorter ones.

Long sentence	Shorter sentences
Organizations that embrace product orientation focus on creating the best quality product possible, rather than carrying out extensive market research at the start of the product's life cycle, but ignoring the needs of the market may lead customers to shop elsewhere and this can affect profits so organizations need to be careful when they take a product-oriented approach.	*Organizations that embrace product orientation focus on creating the best quality product possible, rather than carrying out extensive market research at the start of the product's life cycle. The danger here is that if the organization ignores the needs of the market, customers may shop elsewhere, and the organization's profits may be affected. For this reason, organizations need to be careful when taking a product-oriented approach.*

Table 13.4 An example of one long sentence split into three shorter ones

Be concise

Nobody likes to have to read a whole paragraph of academic waffle just to tease out a simple point that could have been made in one sentence. If you can make your meaning obvious with 50 words rather than 200 then your writing will likely be clearer and more engaging, and your advisor will thank you for it.

The advice here basically comes down to **"use fewer words."** But let's expand on that a little:

- **Use simpler words** where possible (it's a pervasive but incorrect myth that what makes writing "academic" is using a lot of long, complicated words and sentences).
- **Avoid unnecessary repetition.** Cut words, phrases, or whole paragraphs that repeat something you've already said.
- **Stay on topic.** Make sure everything you say is relevant and supports your point. Ask yourself: does this contribute to my argument? If it doesn't, leave it out (even if it took you ages to research, or you think it's really interesting).
- Leave yourself plenty of time to **rewrite and edit your work.** Expressing complex ideas clearly and concisely is hard, and often doesn't happen the first time. Often you'll only notice how to tighten up your sentences once you come back to them and start rewriting and editing.
- One way to tighten up your sentences is to **avoid unnecessary words and phrases** that don't add anything to the meaning. Sometimes these can be hard to spot because we use filler words and phrases automatically, but it's a good thing to look out for when rewriting and editing. For example, replace "Ahmed makes the argument that" with "Ahmed argues that"; "A greater salt intake was

found to increase" with "A greater salt intake increased"; and "An example of this is" with "For example."

- Remember that you can use **acronyms and initialisms** (shortened versions of names and other specialist terms) that are accepted in formal writing, such as "NATO" for the North Atlantic Treaty Organization. Just make sure it's clear what these acronyms or initialisms stand for. For example, when you first introduce the CIA you could say "The Central Intelligence Agency (CIA) was formed in 1947," then all the following mentions of the agency could just refer to "the CIA."

 **Tip!**

As with most writing advice, guidelines like these are nuanced and don't always apply. Sometimes longer words express exactly what you want to say. Sometimes repetition can help to reiterate an important point and help your readers to remember it. Sometimes words and phrases that aren't "necessary" add life to writing and improve its flow. So, remember that there are always exceptions.

Table 13.5 gives one example of how a paragraph can be edited down so it's more concise.

Longer paragraph	More concise version
Start-ups represent an increasingly common form of business. Typically, start-ups are identified by the following features: they are new businesses that have not been operating for very long; they aim to grow relatively quickly; and they tend to take a less traditional and more flexible approach to doing business than other companies that have been established for a long time.	*Start-ups are becoming more common. Typically, start-ups are new businesses that aim to grow quickly. They are also often less traditional and more flexible in their approach.*

Table 13.5 An example of a paragraph rewritten more concisely

Be cautious

Academia is fundamentally based on caution. It progresses in tiny, tentative steps: theories are cautiously proposed, then tested and criticized by others, and gradually academics tiptoe forward in their quest to try to work out what is *true* while always recognizing that the truth is very, very hard to obtain.

It's rare to be one hundred percent sure that something is right or wrong, and academic writing needs to reflect this. Being cautious will also help your reader trust what you've got to say (because if they think you're exaggerating, they won't trust you're telling the truth).

Here are some ways to show caution in your writing:

- **Try not to generalize.** Be careful of using terms that suggest things are always a certain way: "This research shows that X *never* happens," "Graduates *always* earn more," "Y *definitely* leads to Z." But be careful here: there are also more subtle ways to generalize. "Christians go to church" is a generalization because while many Christians do go to church, not all of them do. So a more cautious (and precise) statement would be "Many Christians go to church" or "Christians may go to church."
- **Be careful of words that may exaggerate or overstate:** "Riley's results are *really* persuasive," "Gordon's study is *extremely* unclear," "The protest was *very* successful."
- **Use hedging language.** These are words or phrases that express caution or uncertainty, such as *suggest*, *appears*, *seems*, *might*, *could*, *possibly*, *probably*, etc.
- **Admit to limitations.** This is a time-honored approach in academia. By admitting the limitations in your research, it shows you're aware of the bigger context and have an objective understanding of what your research can achieve.

However, it's important to remember that with your thesis you're trying to create an argument, and you need to commit to that argument. You want your reader to get to the end of what you've written and be convinced by what you've said. So sometimes you'll want to assert your views with more certainty. Don't be afraid of doing this if you think it's warranted; just be careful that the claims you're making seem fair.

Here's an example.

"This study *proves* that eating ultra-processed foods leads to obesity."

This is too certain. It presents "ultra-processed foods lead to obesity" as fact, and it's highly unlikely that one study by itself can definitively prove this. (Plus, what about all the people who eat ultra-processed foods but don't become obese?)

Let's say the study was small and badly designed, and other research doesn't back it up. This might call for a more cautious approach:

"This study *suggests* that eating ultra-processed foods can lead to obesity."

But perhaps the study was well designed, with a large sample, and it correlates with other findings. It's integral to a central part of your argument. This calls for a more confident approach:

"This study *strongly supports* the hypothesis that eating ultra-processed foods *often contributes* to obesity."

Be precise

Following on closely from the ideas of being clear and cautious is the need to be precise. If you can write with precision, the reader won't have to guess what you mean, and they'll be less likely to misunderstand you. You'll also be more persuasive because it'll be harder to challenge what you've got to say.

In general, being more precise means being **more specific**. Sometimes this involves adding extra details, and sometimes it involves rewording a sentence to remove ambiguity.

The use of **discipline-specific terminology** can also help here. Overusing such terminology can contribute to academic writing coming across as complicated and obscure, but this terminology can also act as a precise, concise shorthand for specialist concepts. For example, it's more precise to say "baptized" than "became a Christian," or "the stakeholders" than "the people with an interest in the company."

Table 13.6 gives a few examples of how sentences can be reworded so they are more precise.

Vague	More precise
At the Yalta Conference toward the end of World War II, the world leaders had different aims.	At the Yalta Conference in February 1945, the Allied leaders disagreed in their approach to Germany.
Around half of the people who completed the survey were positive about reforming the monarchy.	47% of people who completed the survey agreed with the statement that "the monarchy should be reformed so the monarch is no longer the head of the Church."
The initial funds for the business were gathered from many sources: people donating money online, and wealthy individuals who expected to get something in return for their investment.	The seed money for the business came from crowdfunding through Kickstarter, and from business angels.

Table 13.6 Examples of rewording vague sentences in a more precise way

You also want to make sure it's clear what you're referring to when you use pronouns like *it*, *this*, *that*, and *they*. You can find a couple of examples in Table 13.7 (see page 193 in Chapter 16 for more).

Ambiguous	More precise
Research from the Institute for Fiscal Studies shows that more families in the UK are falling into poverty. Unfortunately, **it** has not been widely reported in the media. What does "it" refer to? Is it the Institute for Fiscal Studies, or their research, or just the general fact that more families are falling into poverty?	Research from the Institute for Fiscal Studies shows that more families in the UK are falling into poverty. Unfortunately, **this research** has not been widely reported in the media.
One difference between children today and children in the 1990s is that **they** spend more time on social media. Does "they" refer to children today or children in the 1990s?	One difference between children today and children in the 1990s is that **children today** spend more time on social media.

Table 13.7 Examples of rewording ambiguous sentences in a more precise way

Finally, remember that it is important to use precision when describing quantity (see Table 13.8 for examples).

Vague	More precise
The organization's profits dropped.	The organization's annual profits dropped significantly, from $3.5m to $1.3m.
The pH of the solution was high.	The pH of the solution was 12.5.

Table 13.8 Examples of describing quantity in a more precise way

Be objective

Your advisor cares about what you think. They want *your* opinions and reflections to shape the central argument you're putting forward in your thesis. But they also expect you to write objectively, so your writing isn't skewed by personal beliefs or feelings.

This might sound contradictory, but it is possible to get your opinions across in an objective, unbiased way. It basically means constructing an argument **using**

evidence and reasoning, which we'll look at in more detail in Chapter 14. But as a simple example, it's the difference between writing *"I think more houses for low-income families should be built,"* and *"This research supports the idea that building more affordable houses would improve the lives of low-income families."*

Writing objectively also means **not letting your personal beliefs and feelings show**, even if it's a subject you're passionate about. You can find a couple of examples in Table 13.9.

Too subjective	More objective
Margaret Thatcher was a cold-hearted prime minister.	Margaret Thatcher was regarded by many as a cold-hearted prime minister, for example because of her response to the 1984 miners' strike.
Because of greedy fossil fuel companies and short-sighted world leaders, the climate crisis will lead to a depressingly broken world that is much worse than the one we live in today.	The scientific consensus is that fossil fuel emissions are a leading contributor to global warming (see for example Romney's 2021 meta-analysis). Humanity's tendency to focus on the short term (Tanaka, 2012), coupled with political systems where leaders only expect to be in charge for a short period of time (such as in the USA and UK), have also contributed to a lack of progress toward reducing global warming. The effects of this will be significant. For example, scientists have predicted that by 2050, food production will have deteriorated to the point where it will not be possible to feed the global population (Murphy, 2020).

Table 13.9 Examples of rewording subjective sentences in a more objective way

You'll notice that the rewritten version of the climate crisis paragraph is much longer. This is partly because it's using more formal, objective language (removing words like *greedy*, *short-sighted*, and *depressingly*). But it's also because while it's essentially making the same points as the original paragraph, it's supporting those points with evidence. It's making the same claim but arguably in a more persuasive way (despite the lack of emotive language), because it's supported by research results.

A final way to show objectivity is by **giving a balanced viewpoint**. This means considering ideas and arguments that disagree with what you're saying. If you can acknowledge these conflicting viewpoints, and then go on to explain why they can be refuted, your writing (and overall argument) will become stronger.

Thesis writing summary #13

- **Be formal.** Avoid using "I" (unless you've agreed on this with your advisor). Write in complete sentences, avoiding casual language, contractions, and more informal ways of writing.
- **Be clear.** Write shorter sentences where possible, and make sure your point is clear.
- **Be concise.** Cut down your sentences by, for example, avoiding repetition, using simpler language, and editing your writing to remove unnecessary words and phrases.
- **Be cautious.** Be more tentative in your writing when you are less convinced by something (for example by using hedging language); be more confident when you are convinced by something and it is an important part of your central argument.
- **Be precise.** Make sure the meaning of your sentences is unambiguous by using precise and specific language.
- **Be objective.** Avoid using subjective or emotional language. Instead, use evidence and reasoning to persuade the reader of your argument.

How to build up an argument

A good thesis will always have an overarching **argument**. This means the different parts of the thesis are well connected as each new part logically builds on what came before. There should be a "golden thread" that drives your thesis forward toward your conclusions and recommendations (see Chapter 11), and allows you to provide an answer to your original research question (see Chapter 5). In this chapter, we're going to look at constructing an argument from the ground up, one sentence or paragraph at a time.

We'll start with a fundamental building block of good writing, and talk about how to write effective sentences. We'll then look at how to combine and link those sentences together to create well-structured paragraphs. Finally, we'll talk about how to incorporate evidence and critical analysis into your paragraphs to build up an argument.

Let's start with one of the smallest building blocks of your thesis: sentences.

How to write sentences

Sentences vary so much that it's hard to give general advice about how to write "good" ones. But let's talk about two general principles that are useful starting points.

Sentences should be clear

Each sentence should make **one basic point** (although you can qualify and expand on that point within the sentence, as we've done here in brackets).

The meaning of each sentence needs to be clear. A good way to test this is to **read the sentence out loud**. Did it make sense to you? If you get to the end of the sentence and you're not really sure what you just read—you can't easily pinpoint what it was trying to say—it's a sign that the sentence is probably too long or complex.

Here are a few ways to make sentences clearer (see also Chapter 13):

- Try **rewriting** the sentence to make sure the main point is expressed clearly. Take a moment to ask yourself "What do I really mean?" (see page 155), and make sure the answer to that question comes across plainly in your writing. (Rewriting is a core part of good writing; many professional writers spend longer rewriting their sentences than getting them down on paper in the first place.)

- Try **splitting the sentence up** into shorter sentences, or using punctuation (probably commas) to break up different phrases. Read the sentence out loud again and notice where you want to pause or take a breath; that's probably where to break up the sentence. Or check to see if there's more than one basic point or idea in the sentence. If so, split the ideas up into separate sentences.
- Longer sentences tend to be clearer when the **subject and verb are closer together**. This just makes it easier for the reader to process the important information in the sentence (who the sentence is talking about and what they're doing). Two examples are given in Table 14.1.

Subject and verb too far apart	Subject and verb closer together
The solution's pH [subject], *after adding 2ml of hydrochloric acid, increased* [verb] *in acidity by 30%.*	*The solution's pH* [subject] *increased* [verb] *in acidity by 30% after adding 2ml of hydrochloric acid.*
The organization [subject], *after consulting with various stakeholders (including the local community, who overwhelmingly approved the idea following a town hall meeting), introduced* [verb] *a circular business model.*	*The organization* [subject] *introduced* [verb] *a circular business model after consulting with various stakeholders, including the local community. The local community overwhelmingly approved the idea following a town hall meeting.*

Table 14.1 Examples of subject and verb too far apart and closer together

Longer sentences also tend to be clearer when the ideas within them **unfold in a logical and clear manner**. You can think of the sentence as a (tiny) story where you're taking the reader on a journey: the sentence needs to unfold in an order that makes sense. Does the sentence jump around between a number of unrelated points? Or is there a clear progression of thought within it?

Here's a sentence that doesn't work very well:

> *Hamlet was poorly received by critics, although the play had a relatively modest budget, whereas the director for The Tempest changed the setting of the banquet in Act 3.*

This sentence includes three seemingly unrelated points: it's not clear why *Hamlet* was poorly received by critics (was it the modest budget or something else?), or why the information about *The Tempest* is relevant.

Let's look at another example:

The play was poorly received by critics who were unimpressed by Rosen's portrayal of Hamlet, which the critics considered to be less nuanced and charismatic than Omar's performance the previous season.

This sentence works better as it follows a **logical train of thought**, unfolding to give further explanation and more detail:

- The play was poorly received.
- Why?
- Because critics were unimpressed with Rosen.
- Why?
- Because his performance was worse than Omar's.

Sentences should be complete and grammatically correct

As we noted on page 153, academic writing is formal in style and this means sentences need to be complete and grammatically correct.

We don't want to get hopelessly tangled in the principles of English grammar here (that's what Chapter 16 is for!), so let's just stick to some general advice on how to spot and correct grammar mistakes (and to what extent you should be worrying about this).

One of the hardest things to know is *when* you're making grammar mistakes. This is where it can really help to have **personalized feedback** on your writing. You could check through any feedback on your earlier work (such as your essays over the past year), and make a note of any grammar problems that keep popping up. Or you could ask your advisor to read some of your writing and make a note of any major/recurring grammar problems. Your university may offer free, personalized writing support, such as one-to-one tutorials. Or try asking a relative or friend who likes grammar!

Once you know what type of mistakes you're more likely to make, you can look these up in Chapter 16, a good grammar book or online. Figure out how to fix the mistakes, then make a note to watch out for them in your own writing.

Once you've written your thesis, it can help to have a **dedicated editing phase** (see Chapter 17), where you read back over everything and look out for anything that doesn't quite seem right.

 **Tip!**

Grammar checkers (such as Word's built-in grammar checker, or more sophisticated grammar-checking software like Grammarly or ProWritingAid) may be helpful here but bear in mind that they're not always right. Where they can be useful is in identifying issues, so you've got an idea of what might be wrong and can look this up elsewhere.

Remember that **clarity matters more than grammatical accuracy**. There are some grammar mistakes that will affect the meaning of a sentence and definitely make it harder to understand. But there are others that won't matter so much. There are grammar "preferences" that can be ignored and it's not the end of the world.

For example, one grammar preference in academic writing is that you shouldn't start a sentence with "and" or "but," but we've done that throughout this book (such as in the paragraph above), and it hasn't made the writing any less clear. So it'd be far better to spend your limited time reviewing your writing to make sure it actually makes sense and your overall argument is clear and well-structured, rather than combing through every sentence to reword any starting with "and" or "but."

Rather than trying to make sure every sentence you write is grammatically perfect, and spending hours and hours trying to master English grammar, focus your efforts: try to make sure your sentences, above all else, are clear (see above); try to work out which (more important) grammar mistakes you make most often; then make a note of those issues, learn how to fix them, and try to avoid them when you write (and look out for them when you're editing).

Let's move on now to the next building block of writing: paragraphs.

How to write paragraphs

A paragraph is a group of sentences that **develop one main idea or point**. Each paragraph should take your reader one step forward in your argument.

Paragraphs help to break up your writing so it's less tiring to read. At the end of each paragraph, your reader can pause and take a little rest, then move on to the next one. Paragraphs also help to give your writing structure, by guiding your reader through the development of your ideas.

In a nonfiction book like this one, it's OK for paragraphs to be one or two sentences long. But paragraphs this short should usually be avoided in your thesis. Instead, a good length to aim for is 100 to 250 words.

An academic paragraph should typically include the following three elements.

(This is certainly not the only way to structure paragraphs in academic writing, and you shouldn't feel shackled to it, but it's a useful guide.)

1. **The opening sentence** (known as the "topic sentence"), which introduces or outlines your point.
2. **Supporting sentences**, which allow you to develop your point with evidence, explanations, or examples. This is where you add more detail to explain or support your point.
3. **The concluding sentence**, which may link your point to your overall argument (if this is appropriate). Or it could simply round off the paragraph, or hint at what the next paragraph is about.

The main thing to remember here is that each paragraph **introduces and then develops one point**. Each sentence within the paragraph needs to be relevant to that point.

Paragraphs also need to have a **logical structure**. Earlier in this chapter we said you can think of longer sentences as being like a tiny story unfolding; the same is true of paragraphs, just on a slightly larger scale. The points need to flow or unfold in a logical way. A few ways to order your points include:

- by time (describing events in the order they happen)
- by detail (starting with the big picture, then going into the details)
- by cause and effect (showing how one thing leads to another).

If you're not sure whether a paragraph or section of text is ordered sensibly, a good question to ask is: **what does the reader need to know for this to make sense?** Then make sure that information has already appeared. Think of a cake recipe. You wouldn't tell someone to put the cake in the oven without first turning the oven on, or to ice the cake before first letting it cool down. The recipe has a logical order; a good paragraph does too.

Using fictitious citations to show you how to incorporate evidence, here's an example of a well-structured paragraph:

*[**Topic sentence:**] Rodriguez (2009) argues that companies hoping to improve staff performance should first focus on staff retention. [**Supporting sentences, including reasoning and evidence:**] This is because he believes it is easier, quicker, and cheaper to upskill current staff rather than recruit and train new staff. However, while it is possible for a company to quantify how much time and money they have saved by upskilling rather than recruiting, it is harder to prove that increased staff retention in itself improves performance. For example, Rodriguez cites the example of a small environmental charity struggling to retain employees; when the charity increased its employees' salaries and encouraged a better work–life balance, staff retention*

*improved by 23% over the following 6 months, and a year later productivity had risen by 14% (Clement, 2005). Rodriguez acknowledges that it is hard to determine what caused the increase in productivity: it may have been the increased retention, but it could have also been as a result of the better work–life balance or other policies the company introduced to improve retention. [**Concluding sentence:**] This ambiguity suggests that a strategy to improve staff performance needs to be multifaceted, encompassing a range of changes in the workplace.*

The supporting and concluding sentences are where you introduce critical analysis. We'll look at this more on pages 171–174, where we'll talk about how you can use your paragraphs to build up an argument.

Signposting

Signposts help to make sure someone on a journey doesn't get lost; they guide us through the landscape and warn us about what's coming up. Signposting in academic writing basically does the same thing. It helps you to link the building blocks of sentences and paragraphs together to create writing that flows well. It also helps the reader to follow your arguments by making it clearer how points are connected.

Signposts can be **individual "linking" words**. You can use them to signal how sentences relate to each other and to indicate to the reader where you're taking them next. They can also help to build up your argument and create a clear structure. Some common ones can be found in Table 14.2.

Word or phrase	Used...	Example
In contrast *Alternatively* *However*	To make a different/opposing point; to mean "regardless of this" or "in spite of this"	The prime minister's speech was measured and calm. However, it did not soothe the financial markets.
Furthermore *In addition* *Moreover*	To add a supporting point/ build up an argument	The study claimed that a plant-based diet increased life expectancy. Furthermore, it claimed that this diet could reduce the risk of dementia.
For example *In particular* *Specifically*	To go into more detail	The drought severely affected the farmers in the region. In particular, it impacted those with large herds of cattle to feed.
Therefore *As a result* *Consequently*	To summarize a point/ show reasoning/show a consequence	The start-up failed to secure further funding. As a result, it collapsed after nine months of trading.

Table 14.2 Examples of commonly used "linking" words

 **Tip!**

Be careful that you're using linking words appropriately and with some restraint (you don't need them everywhere!). For example, if a sentence is going to start with "Alternatively" then it really does need to be making a contrasting point to the previous one. If a sentence is going to start with "Furthermore" then it really does need to build on the previous one. If your sentences simply don't connect well in the first place then throwing in a bunch of linking words won't fix that.

You can also signpost structure to show how the bit you're currently writing fits in with the rest of the thesis. This helps the reader to orient themselves in your overall argument, and it helps to make the structure of your thesis clear. You can use signposting to show how your writing links back to something that's already been said, or to indicate what's coming up. Again, you don't want to go overboard with this, but used occasionally it can help to make your whole thesis feel more coherent (see Table 14.3 for a few examples).

Phrases to refer backward	Phrases to refer forward
• *"As the previous study showed …"* • *"In contrast to the previous approach …"* • *"Using the method outlined earlier …"* • *"Referring back to Hidayat's argument …"*	• *"As the following example shows …"* • *"Evidence to support this argument includes …"* • *"…, which will be demonstrated later in this study"* • *"This will be discussed further in the next chapter."*

Table 14.3 Examples of phrases to refer backward and forward

How to build an argument

We've seen that academic paragraphs usually start with an opening sentence, followed by supporting sentences. What should the supporting sentences consist of? The answer to that depends on the purpose of the paragraph, but they could cover a whole range of things: explaining a concept, describing a process, summarizing a theory, analyzing evidence, and more. Let's look here in particular at how to use those supporting sentences to build up an argument, using evidence and critical analysis of that evidence.

Critical writing

Descriptive writing is where you're describing or informing the reader about something: for example, describing a research method, or explaining a concept, or summarizing previous research.

This type of writing is important. You'll need to use it in your thesis to, for example, describe previous research as part of the *Literature Review*, or describe the methods and results of your own research. But you also need to build on it with **critical writing**.

Critical writing doesn't mean simply disagreeing with everyone and trying to find flaws in their ideas. It means building up an argument that is based on reasoning and evidence, so you can persuade the reader of your point of view.

At its core, critical writing is based on **asking questions**. Rather than just accepting everything you read, you need to ask questions like:

- How does this research build on previous research?
- Is this study reliable? Why or why not?
- Is this author's argument persuasive? Why or why not?
- What can be learned from this? How can the findings be used?
- How does this research weaken or strengthen my overall argument?

Addressing these types of questions in your writing is basically what we mean by **critical analysis**. In effect, you're analyzing evidence (judging how useful/relevant/reliable etc. it is) in a critical way (through objective, careful questioning).

Mini arguments

Your whole thesis will have an overarching argument, which you can think of as being built from lots of "mini" arguments. Each mini argument should include the following:

- A **claim**
- A **reason** to support that claim
- **Evidence** to support the reason
- **Critical analysis** of that evidence.

As you're writing your thesis, you can think of the mini argument as your response to a reader sitting just behind your shoulder saying "Why?", "Prove it!", and "So what?":

- **Why?** What is the reason for your claim?
- **Prove it!** Show me the evidence that supports your reason.
- **So what?** Why is this important? Why are you telling me this?

Here's an example of how to build up a mini argument using these elements (all the citations are invented).

Claim: *Another factor that can affect children's learning in school is hunger.*

Why *(does hunger affect children's learning)?*

Reason: *Without the energy provided by food, children lose concentration and motivation, making it harder for them to focus on their learning.*

Prove it!

Evidence: *Scientific studies have shown that hunger is linked to lower blood sugar levels, which leads to fatigue and reduced energy (Dart, 2015; Joules, 2008). Similarly, scientific studies have shown that the ability to concentrate and take in new information is impaired by tiredness (Zhao, 2018).*

So what?

Link to overall argument: *As with the factors discussed previously (particularly the extent to which parents are involved in their children's learning), hunger is another area that teachers have little control over. This contributes to the argument that teachers should not be penalized for the poor exam results of the children they teach.*

These sentences could form a complete paragraph, but it would be missing any critical analysis of the evidence. So we could expand the "Prove it!" section as follows (the bits of critical analysis are in bold):

*Scientific studies have shown that hunger is linked to lower blood sugar levels, which leads to fatigue and reduced energy (Dart, 2015; Joules, 2008). Similarly, scientific studies have shown that the ability to concentrate and take in new information is impaired by tiredness (Zhao, 2018). **For ethical reasons it is implausible to devise a study to try to prove that hunger affects learning in the classroom, as it would require intentionally withholding food from children.** However, various longitudinal studies have suggested a strong link between persistent hunger in childhood and health problems including fatigue (Boucher, 2020; Szymanek, 1996). **While these studies cannot prove a causal relationship, they add weight to the theory that hunger negatively affects learning.***

Here's another example of a (fictitious) mini argument that could form a complete paragraph, based on the key sentence types we explored above (again, the bits of critical analysis are in bold):

Topic sentence (claim): *In 2018, the local government in Cuzco argued that the number of people allowed to hike the Inca Trail in Peru should be reduced by half, from 500 each day to 250 each day.*

Supporting sentences (reason, evidence, critical analysis of that evidence):

*They believed this would limit the environmental degradation along the trail. This was **supported by** Diaz (2015), who found that the variety and frequency of plant and animal species along the trail had reduced noticeably over a 5-year-period, **although Diaz does not say if a similar degradation has also occurred in the surrounding area; if this is the case then the degradation may not be the result of hikers on the trail but due to wider environmental trends.** In response to the proposals to restrict the trail, Featherwear (2019) interviewed 20 sherpas who regularly walk the trail and they agreed that the local environment has degraded over the past decades, but most did not think this was because of trail use. However, **it is possible the sherpas would be reluctant to blame hikers for this situation because their livelihoods (and their families) depend on the trail remaining open.***

Concluding sentence (linking the paragraph to a broader argument):

This highlights how difficult it can be to balance tourism and conservation, with conflicting priorities between protecting livelihoods today versus the environment (and by extension, livelihoods) tomorrow.

Of course it wouldn't be appropriate to follow this format for every paragraph in your thesis, but consider using it when you're trying to put forward evidence or convince your reader of something. Let's now take a quick look at how to weave such evidence into your writing.

Incorporating evidence

There are essentially two ways to incorporate evidence into your thesis: you can either quote it directly, or put it into your own words.

Quotes (which repeat the author's exact words) should be used sparingly, as generally an advisor will want to read your own words rather than someone else's (it's your thesis, after all). But quotes can be useful when the original wording is important: perhaps because it has historical significance, or the author has expressed themselves in a unique way, or the way they have defined a concept is notable.

Short quotes should be placed in quote marks within the main body of the paragraph. You should always give the page number of the original quote. For example:

Chao and Chan define euthanasia as "direct intentional killing of a person as part of the medical care being offered" (2002, p. 128); here the intention behind the act distinguishes it from the practice of withdrawing life-sustaining treatment.

Longer quotes (40 words or more in APA style) should sit in their own paragraph, which is indented. Here you don't need to use quote marks. For example:

> Wong et al. (2021) refer to a type of student they call "the naïve," which encompasses those:
>
>> who do not believe issues of race and racism are relevant in contemporary society, especially in the UK. More specifically, racial inequality, prejudice and discrimination are considered to be lessons of history rather than an active or on-going concern. These students accept that racism existed, but only in the past, and are therefore unaware, or deny, that it is still a current issue for social justice. (p. 364)

Quotes should always use the author's exact words, but you can make small edits to them if you indicate what you've done (see Table 14.4).

Technique	Original	Edited
If you want to shorten a quote by cutting irrelevant or unimportant material from it, use an ellipses (three periods with spaces between them in APA style, i.e. " . . . ") to indicate this	"The company's official response, which was posted on Twitter 6 hours after the incident, was brief and unapologetic."	"The company's official response . . . was brief and unapologetic."
If the quote doesn't make sense when taken out of context, and you want to edit it to make the meaning clearer, put your edits in square brackets	"When the breakfast club was cut at school, they were furious and petitioned Mrs Lovett."	"When the breakfast club was cut at school, [the parents] were furious and petitioned Mrs Lovett [the headteacher]."
If there's an error in the quote (such as a misspelling) then you can add "[sic]" to indicate this (so the reader knows the error was in the original quote and you haven't introduced it)	"One survey respondent wrote that 'I was comple-mented by my line manager for my excellent work.'"	"One survey respondent wrote that 'I was comple-mented [sic] by my line manager for my excellent work.'"
If there are particular words you want to emphasize in the quote (to draw the reader's attention to them), you can put them in italics or bold and add "[emphasis added]"	"The company's shift to remote working was poorly planned and made it harder for new starters to integrate into the team."	"The company's shift to remote working was poorly planned and **made it harder for new starters to integrate into the team** [emphasis added]."

Table 14.4 Examples of making small edits in quotes

Rather than quoting from sources directly, most of the time you'll want to rewrite information **in your own words** (also known as **"paraphrasing"**). For example, you might want to summarize an author's argument, describe the research they carried out, or critique their findings. You should still reference the source (though you won't need to include a specific page number as you would with a quote).

The danger here is that it can be quite easy to plagiarize. This is an important issue, and you can find more detailed information about how to avoid plagiarism in Chapter 15.

Let's finish this chapter with a few tips on what type of evidence to use in your thesis:

- Use **high-quality evidence** to support your arguments. Pages 32–34 in Chapter 4 give some advice on what counts as "high-quality" academic literature. Consider, for example: the age of the research (is older research now outdated?), whether the research has been peer-reviewed and published by a reputable journal/publisher, and whether the methodology behind the research is sound.
- Use **relevant evidence** to support your arguments. Only include evidence if it relates to the point you're making. Pages 34–36 in Chapter 4 talk about how to find relevant evidence.
- **Don't just ignore all evidence that goes against your argument** and pretend it doesn't exist. Consider this evidence in your thesis but show why your argument stands strong anyway.

Thesis writing summary #14

- **Aim to write sentences that are clear, complete, and grammatically correct.** Try to make sure your sentences are well-structured and they don't use overly complex language, so your meaning comes across clearly. Each sentence should make one basic point.
- **Aim to write well-structured paragraphs that develop one basic idea.** Most of your paragraphs will likely be 100 to 250 words long, and consist of a topic sentence, supporting sentences, and a concluding sentence.
- **Use signposts (linking words and phrases) to connect your sentences and paragraphs together.** These help to add structure to your writing.
- **Incorporate evidence and critical analysis of that evidence into your writing.** Each "mini argument" you write should include a claim, a reason for that claim, evidence to support the reason, and critical analysis of the evidence. Build on your descriptive writing with critical writing.
- **Either quote evidence directly or put it into your own words.** Aim to use high-quality, relevant evidence to support your arguments.

How to use references
and avoid plagiarism

"If I have seen further it is by standing on the shoulder of giants,"[1] wrote Sir Isaac Newton. What's true for one of the most influential scientists in human history is even more true for the rest of us. Good scientific work never starts from scratch. It always builds on the ideas and findings developed and discovered by other researchers.

When we build on the work of others in a thesis (which we definitely should do—especially in the *Introduction*, *Literature Review*, and *Discussion*), we also need to give them adequate credit. We do so by referencing their work.

Using citation styles to incorporate evidence

As we've discussed in Chapter 14, there are **two basic ways to incorporate evidence in your thesis: quotes** (where you reproduce the texts of others word for word) and **paraphrasing** (where you use your own words to describe facts, ideas, or thoughts that are taken from another source). In both cases, you need to add a citation, thereby giving credit to the original author.

What a citation looks like depends on the **citation style** that your university is using. The most common ones are **APA** (American Psychological Association) style, used primarily in psychology, education, business, and social sciences; **MLA** (Modern Language Association) style, which is widely used in the humanities; and **Chicago style** (used in several disciplines).

Some universities also use their own "house style." Some prefer in-text citations (including the author's name and year of publication directly in the body of the text). Others prefer this information to be given in footnotes (at the bottom of the page) or endnotes (at the end of the chapter or document). Check out the citation standards and requirements of your institution. If in doubt, ask your advisor for guidance.

Table 15.1 includes some **examples of references in the widely used APA style** (see also Appendix 1, which includes a more detailed guide to APA style for referencing).

Type of source	Citation in text	In the list of references
Book	Sternad (2019) argues that this is "even more true for the rest of us" (p. 34). [This is also called a narrative citation, as it is directly integrated into the narrative.] "Good scientific work never starts from scratch" (Sternad, 2019, p. 34). [This is an example of a citation in parentheses after the sentence.]	Sternad, D. (2019). *Effective management: Developing yourself, others and organizations.* Red Globe Press.
Book chapter (from an edited book)	[Narrative citation:] Sternad and Mödritscher (2021) ... [Citation in parentheses after the sentence:] (Sternad & Mödritscher, 2021).	Sternad, D., & Mödritscher, G. (2021). Qualitative growth: An alternative to solely quantitatively-oriented theories of firm growth. In M. Pirson, D. M. Wasieleski, & E. L. Stickler (Eds.), *Alternative Theories of the Firm* (pp. 103–119). Routledge. https://doi.org/10.4324/9781003211549
Journal article	[Narrative citation:] Pittino et al. (2016) ... [Citation in parentheses after the sentence:] (Pittino et al., 2016).	Pittino, D., Visintin, F., Lenger, T., & Sternad, D. (2016). Are high performance work practices really necessary in family SMEs? An analysis of the impact on employee retention. *Journal of Family Business Strategy, 7*(2), 75–89. https://doi.org/10.1016/j.jfbs.2016.04.002
Webpage (individual authors)	[Narrative citation:] Bradley et al. (2016) ... [Citation in parentheses after the sentence:] (Bradley et al., 2016).	Bradley, F., Sternad, D., & Kennelly, J. (2017, March 4). *It's time to measure business success beyond profit.* https://www.greenbiz.com/article/its-time-measure-business-success-beyond-profit
Webpage (organizational)	[Narrative citation:] World Trade Organization (2022) ... [Citation in parentheses after the sentence:] (World Trade Organization, 2022).	World Trade Organization. (2022, February 24). *WTO chairpersons for 2022.* https://www.wto.org/english/news_e/pres22_e/pr898_e.htm

Table 15.1 Examples of references in APA style

Tip!

If you use Google Scholar for searching for academic literature, you can export references in different citation styles when you click on "Cite" under the search result. Be careful and re-check the export data of the citation manually, however, as it is not always 100 percent accurate and complete.

Consider the following **good practices for integrating ideas from other sources** into your text:

- Familiarize yourself with your institution's **style guide** before starting to work on your thesis.
- When conducting your research, **note down the bibliographic details** of each source you use straight away (following the style guide). You can use citation management software like EndNote here, or just a separate document where you collect all of your references (which is usually the faster way).
- If you copy text from a source into your notes, make sure to always put direct quotes in quotation marks (and include the page number of the source where the quote was taken from). This will help you ensure that you do not risk **unintentional plagiarism** when you cannot remember later on whether a paragraph in your notes was a direct quote or paraphrased.
- Cite in such a way that the reader knows, **sentence by sentence**, exactly what's your own work (without citation), where you've included ideas from others in your own words (paraphrasing, cited), and where you directly quote the work of others (in quotation marks, cited with a page number). Make sure that each sentence is clearly attributable. Just citing at the end of a paragraph is usually not enough.
- **Avoid an overuse of direct quotes.** A thesis should be *your* paper, with your own voice, not just a string of quotes. It is thus advisable to use direct quotes only very selectively.
- **Re-check your list of references before you hand in your thesis.** Don't give your advisor the impression that you are lazy. Proofread your references— check if you correctly followed all the guidelines, including, for example, using italics for titles, the correct use of capital letters, and the correct use of punctuation.

As well as citing text that is based on external sources, you should also cite **graphs, figures, and tables** that are based on the work of others. The style guide you're using should tell you how to label and cite them. The citation requirements will vary based on whether you use an exact copy of the original or an adapted version.

How to avoid plagiarism

The word **"plagiarism"** can spark a lot of anxiety in graduate students. You might have heard about cases of important people who have lost their jobs due to being accused of plagiarizing in their graduate thesis or dissertation. (Two former German ministers, Theodor zu Guttenberg and Annette Schavan, are prominent examples here.)

The word "plagiarism" stems from the Latin "plagiarius," which means "kidnapper." People who plagiarize kidnap the ideas of others, presenting them as if they were their own without giving proper credit to the original source.

The most audacious way of plagiarizing is to just take whole chunks of text from another source, copy it into yours, and then "forget" to cite it, so readers get the impression that the words are your own. Most students understand why and how to avoid this, but may struggle with less obvious forms of plagiarism. Let's take a look at these now, to help you avoid inadvertent or "accidental" plagiarizing.

As a basic rule, if you're putting a chunk of someone else's text into your own words, you can't just change a few words and leave it at that: you'll need to rewrite the text more completely so you retain the original meaning but put it into your own words and sentences.

If you're finding this hard to do, one tip is to read the original source, put it away so you can't see it, then try to rewrite it in your own words. Or read the source, ask yourself what it's really saying, summarize this out loud to yourself, and *then* write that down.

Table 15.2 includes an example of a quote that has been rewritten twice; the first rewrite could constitute plagiarism, while the second rewrite is different enough to the original to be safe.

The quote that was too similar to the original in Table 15.2 is an example of **mosaic plagiarism**. That's basically bad paraphrasing, where you change a few words of a sentence, but still "borrow" several of the phrases and maybe also the sentence structure from the original source. Even if you cite this type of patchwork sentence (without quotation marks), it's still not OK from a plagiarism perspective.

Original text	*"Good mental health and life satisfaction are important for fostering a flourishing and prosperous society. Therefore, creating the conditions that promote good long-term mental health has increasingly become ... a priority for schools—so much so that parents may look at pastoral support as a consideration in selecting an appropriate school for their child." (Henderson et al., 2022)*
Too similar to the original (same wording as in the original text highlighted in bold)	*Henderson et al. (2022) argue that positive **mental health and life satisfaction are** vital **for a flourishing and** happy **society**. As a result, **creating the conditions that promote good mental health** in the long term **has increasingly become a priority for schools**, to the extent that **parents may** consider **pastoral support** when choosing **an appropriate school for their child.***
Different enough	*Henderson et al. (2022) argue that a society cannot flourish without good mental health. Schools and parents are increasingly coming to understand this and are prioritizing pastoral support more as a result.*

Table 15.2 An example of rewriting a quote with and without the risk of plagiarism

In addition to direct plagiarism ("copying and pasting" text from elsewhere without citations) and mosaic plagiarism, there are some other common forms of plagiarism:

- **Paraphrasing without citing the source:** this is taking an idea from another person and writing it in your own words, but not including a citation for the original idea.
- **Follow-up plagiarism:** this is when you correctly cite one sentence, but then forget to cite the following sentences, even though they also refer to ideas that stem from the same source as the first sentence. This does not mean that you must always cite several sentences in a row if you take them from the same source. You can use other signposts like *"Sternad and Power (2023) use the following three arguments: First, ... Second, ... The final argument is ..."* or *"The four forms of plagiarism summarized by Sternad and Power (2023) include ..."* (and then use bullet points to describe these four forms without further citations). If you take several sentences (e.g. a whole paragraph) from one source, you just need to make it crystal clear to the reader where they are from, either through citing every sentence or by providing enough context that the reader can clearly distinguish which sentences are based on your own ideas, and which ones are reporting on other people's ideas.

- **Structural plagiarism:** this is when you generally use your own language (which of course is OK), but keep the same structure and arguments as in the original text. That could mean using the same (or only slightly adapted) sub-headings in one chapter, or following another author's argument over several sentences or paragraphs (maybe also citing the same sources) without making it explicit that you are doing so.

Be aware that it is also possible to plagiarize yourself. You shouldn't use parts of your own previous work (e.g. from prior seminar papers) without citing them. There could be an exemption, however, for using parts of your thesis proposal in your final thesis. Check out the rules at your university here, just to be on the safe side.

Now that you know what to be aware of, here are a few tips for **how to avoid falling into the plagiarism trap:**

- Whenever you write something down in your notes based on the ideas of others, make sure you put direct quotes in quotation marks. When you paraphrase, use different words and always add a citation (ideally with a page number, so that you can find the original again if you need to re-check it later on).
- When paraphrasing, in addition to using different words and phrases, change the structure of the sentence or paragraph too.
- Do not follow exactly the same sequence of arguments from another source. Be careful when you are taking notes that you don't unintentionally plagiarize the structure of your source.

Before submitting your thesis, you can also conduct a **plagiarism check** with the help of a software program. Ask your local student organization if they offer such an option, or check out this book's companion website for weblinks to such software (*www.econcise.com/ThesisWriting*).

Thesis writing summary #15

- **Whenever you use ideas from other sources, cite them.** Make it clear for each sentence in your thesis whether it includes only your own original thoughts (without citation), direct quotations (cited and placed in quotation marks) or a paraphrase (cited without quotation marks). Use direct quotes sparingly.
- **Familiarize yourself with your university's style guide.** Learn the basic citation style requirements at the beginning of your thesis project (e.g. how to present in-text or footnote citations, and how to correctly format journal articles, books, book chapters and internet sources in the list of references).
- **Beware of less obvious forms of plagiarism** like mosaic plagiarism (mixing your own words with those from another source) or structural plagiarism (following the same sequence of arguments as in another source).
- **Use proper paraphrasing and citations in your notes during the research phase** to avoid inadvertent plagiarism.

How to fix grammar, punctuation, and spelling issues

People have written whole books on how to use grammar and punctuation correctly, and we simply can't cover everything to do with it here. Instead we'll focus on some of the more common problems that students tend to stumble over in their academic writing, giving a basic overview of each issue. We hope that this will arm you with enough knowledge to understand why you might be tripping up in your writing, so you have a better idea of where to go and what to search for if you need more comprehensive help.

This chapter is split into three sections. The first deals with common grammar problems. The second gives a brief overview of different punctuation marks. The third is a table of words that are commonly confused in academic writing (like *affect* and *effect*, or *complement* and *compliment*), with brief definitions and examples.

Grammar

Active versus passive voice

In a sentence in the active voice, the subject is doing something. In a sentence in the passive voice, the subject becomes the person or thing that is having something done to it:

> Active: *The cat [subject] climbed up the tree.*

> Passive: *The tree [subject] was climbed up by the cat.*

General writing advice is to stick with the active voice as much as possible, because it tends to make sentences easier to understand. This is good advice to follow, but it's also perfectly OK to use the passive voice—particularly when you want to focus on what was done, rather than who did it. For example:

> *The participants were selected using stratified sampling.*

> *The experiment was repeated to gather more accurate data.*

Conditional sentences ("if")

Conditional sentences show that one event depends on another one in some way. They consist of two clauses (or phrases): the "if" clause and the main clause. What can be tricky here is getting the tenses in both clauses right. Here's a brief summary of the four main types of conditional sentence.

Zero conditional sentence: refers to something that is generally true.

✓ *If I **do not tidy** my room, it **is** a mess.*

First conditional sentence: refers to something that will happen in the future.

✓ *If I **finish** my work, I **will go** to the movies.*

Second conditional sentence: refers to something that is unlikely to happen.

✓ *If I **had** $10 million, I **would build** my own swimming pool.*

✓ *If the sample **were** larger, the results **would be** more accurate.*

Third conditional sentence: refers to something that didn't happen in the past, and suggests the results would have been different if it had happened:

✓ *If I **had known** about the roadworks, I **would have driven** a different route.*

✓ *If it **had rained** last week, the plants **would have thrived**.*

There are other variations and combinations, so if you're not sure you've got the tenses correct then look up "conditional sentences" in a good grammar book or online.

Dangling participles

This happens when a participle phrase is not attached to a subject, or is attached to the wrong subject. It results in sentences that are ambiguous or illogical, where it seems like the action of the sentence is being carried out by the wrong person or thing.

It often involves sentences starting with an "-ing" word:

✗ *Sitting in the garden, the sun shone fiercely.* (This makes it sound like the sun was sitting in the garden.)

✓ *While I was sitting in the garden, the sun shone fiercely.*

✗ *Driving far too fast, the toddler in the booster seat was screaming.* (This makes it sound like the toddler was driving.)

✓ *The toddler in the booster seat was screaming because his dad was driving far too fast.*

Faulty parallelism

This happens when different parts of a sentence are similar in meaning but do not have the same grammatical structure. It often occurs in lists:

> ✗ *The research involved selecting participants, creating a survey, gathered responses, and analysis of the results.*

Because the list starts with two "-ing" verbs, it would be better if the last two items in the list followed the same pattern:

> ✓ *The research involved selecting participants, creating a survey, gathering responses, and analyzing the results.*

It's easy for faulty parallelism to creep into longer lists in particular. A trick is to take the phrase introducing the list and check if it works with each item in the list in turn. For example, let's take the sentence "The teacher asked the children to hang up their coats, sitting down on the floor, and pay attention to the story." "The teacher asked the children to … pay attention to the story" makes grammatical sense, but "The teacher asked the children to … sitting down on the floor" doesn't. This needs to change to "The teacher asked the children to … sit down on the floor."

Gender-neutral pronouns

For many years, male pronouns (he/him/his) were used in formal writing to refer to people in general:

> ✗ *In this hospital, a doctor needs to wash **his** hands before **he** begins operating.*

This language excludes other genders (why can't the doctor be female?). A more inclusive approach is to use "his or her" or "he or she":

> ✓ *In this hospital, a doctor needs to wash **his or her** hands before **he or she** begins operating.*

But this is clunky and still not fully inclusive, as it doesn't take into account people who don't identify as either male or female (because they're gender nonconforming or nonbinary, for example). So a more inclusive approach still is to use they/them/their:

✓ *In this hospital, a doctor needs to wash **their** hands before **they** begin operating.*

There's some debate over whether using "they" like this is grammatically "correct" and acceptable in academic writing. The Chartered Institute of Editing and Proofreading in the UK says that it's "perfectly acceptable" and its usage "has a long history."[1] The *Chicago Manual of Style* and *Associated Press Stylebook* (two major style guides in the USA) are more cautious, saying that it's best to reword if possible, although there are instances where singular "they" should definitely be used (such as when referring to someone who identifies with that pronoun).

One way to get around the problem is to make the subject plural:

✓ *In this hospital, **doctors** need to wash **their** hands before **they** begin operating.*

Incomplete sentences (sentence fragments)

In formal academic writing, sentences need to be complete. Sentences are incomplete if they're missing a subject or verb.

This is a sentence:

✓ *Academia matters.*

These aren't:

× *The unhappy clown.* (No verb.)

× *Hated chocolate.* (No subject.)

What's trickier to spot is a sentence that's incomplete because it's a **dependent clause** on its own. (Dependent clauses are phrases that depend on main clauses to make sense.) Dependent clauses start with words like although, where, since, which, that, etc.

× *Which suggests the hypothesis is correct.*

✓ *The results were as expected, which suggests the hypothesis is correct.*

× *Although Davis (2023) disagrees.*

✓ *Wesley (2021) claims that the prisoners were dangerous, although Davis (2023) disagrees.*

Relative clauses

A relative clause is a phrase that gives more information about something. If the information isn't an essential part of the sentence—if it could be removed and the sentence would still make sense—then it goes between commas:

✓ *The electrician, who always arrived on time, knocked promptly on the door.*

If the information is essential to the meaning of the sentence then it doesn't go in commas. Compare these examples:

✗ *Mushrooms, which are poisonous, should not be eaten.*

This implies all mushrooms are poisonous. And removing the relative clause leaves us with "mushrooms should not be eaten," which isn't true: it's only poisonous mushrooms that should not be eaten.

✓ *Mushrooms which are poisonous should not be eaten.*

✗ *Teenagers, who are at least 17 years old, are legally allowed to drive.*

This implies that all teenagers are at least 17 years old. And removing the relative clause leaves us with "teenagers are legally allowed to drive," which isn't true: only teenagers who are old enough are legally allowed to drive.

✓ *Teenagers who are at least 17 years old are legally allowed to drive.*

Subject–verb agreement

If the subject in a sentence is singular, then the verb must be singular. If the subject is plural, the verb must be plural.

This sounds simple, but there are situations where working out subject–verb agreement is surprisingly tricky. We can't cover all situations here, so if you're not sure, look it up. Here are a few examples.

✗ *Eating fruit and drinking water **is** important for staying healthy.*

✓ *Eating fruit and drinking water **are** important for staying healthy.* (The subject is made up of two things—eating fruit and drinking water—so it's plural. That means the verb needs to be plural too.)

✗ *A flock of birds **were** circling the field.*

✓ *A flock of birds **was** circling the field.* ("Flock" is singular, so the verb is also singular.)

✗ *The mother, with her two children, **are** swimming in the pool.*

✓ *The mother, with her two children, **is** swimming in the pool.* (The main clause here is "The mother is swimming in the pool." Both the subject and verb of the main clause are singular.)

Tenses

In academic writing, the **past simple tense** is generally used to describe specific research activities that happened in the past:

> ✓ *Johnston's (2023) study **found** that 20% of children had panic attacks.*

> ✓ *I **conducted** a survey using random sampling.*

The **present simple tense** is used to make general statements, explanations, or interpretations. It focuses on what can be known or inferred now.

> ✓ *Sawney's (2022) research **shows** that small businesses cannot afford to ignore customer service.*

> ✓ *The snowy owl **is** facing extinction.*

Here's an example of using the past tense to describe a specific study, and the present tense to explain the results of that study:

> ✓ *Teka (2021) **conducted** a study that showed an increase in the age of first-time home buyers. This **supports** the idea that homes have become more unaffordable for younger people.*

The **present perfect tense** is another tense commonly used in academic writing. It describes actions that started in the past and are still ongoing or relevant today. In this way it acts as a "bridge" between the past and present. It can be used to introduce a new topic, or to summarize research that's happened in an area.

> ✓ *There **have been** several studies into this question.*

> ✓ *Research **has shown** that lemurs are losing their habitat due to climate change.*

The **future tense** is not often used in academic writing, except when describing research you intend to do. You might use it in your thesis proposal or your *Introduction*, for example.

> ✓ *This thesis **will** investigate how the marketing mix differs between sole traders and other SMEs.*

 **Tip!**

The past simple, present simple, and present perfect tenses are three of the most commonly used tenses in academic writing, but there are others too and their uses can quickly get complicated. If you know you struggle with tenses, find a good grammar reference book or resource online to learn more.

Unclear pronouns

We noted on page 161 that one way to bring clarity to your writing is to make sure that when you use a pronoun (e.g. "it," "she," "which"), it's clear what you're referring to.

✗ *After removing the dirt from the wheelbarrow, the gardener threw it away.* (Did the gardener throw the dirt or the wheelbarrow away?)

✓ *The gardener threw the wheelbarrow away after removing the dirt from it.*

✗ *The footballer refused to sing the national anthem, which his fans loved.* (Did the fans love the national anthem, or the fact the footballer refused to sing it?)

✓ *The footballer refused to sing the national anthem; his fans loved this protest.*

Punctuation

Apostrophes (')

Apostrophes are used in two main ways. The first is in contractions (shortened versions of words):

✓ *can't* (cannot), *it's* (it is), *he'd* (he had), etc.

Contractions should generally be avoided in academic writing: spell out the words in full instead.

Apostrophes are also used to show **possession**. Here the general rule is to add 's to an item to show it belongs to someone or something:

✓ *The girl's dog*

✓ *The children's shoes*

One exception is plural nouns which already end in s. To these, just add an apostrophe after the s that's already there:

✓ *The boys' lunchboxes*

✓ *My parents' house* (the house belonging to both my parents); *my parent's house* (the house belonging to just one parent)

 **Tip!**

"It's" always means "it is" or "it has." "Its" always indicates possession. Check which one to use by seeing if you can replace the word with "it is" or "it has" in a sentence:

✓ *The bird spread its wings* ("the bird spread it is wings" doesn't make sense, so there should be no apostrophe here)

✓ *It's rained a lot today* ("it has rained a lot today" makes sense, so there should be an apostrophe here)

The same trick applies with "who's" and "whose." Can you replace the word in the sentence with "who is" or "who has"? If you can, use "who's." If you can't, use "whose."

Colon (:)

A colon is basically used to **introduce things**. In this sense, it is typically used in three ways:

1. To introduce a list. For example:

   ✓ *The iPhone came in three colors: black, white, and red.*

2. To introduce another element in the text, like an example, a diagram, or a quotation.

   ✓ *Here's a diagram that illustrates this point: [diagram is inserted here]*

3. To connect two ideas, where the first idea leads into or introduces the second one. The colon says, "Here comes something!"² Usually the phrase after the colon elaborates or explains what came before it. For example:

   ✓ *The route for the hike was daunting: a steep descent followed by boggy marshland.*

   ✓ *Above all else, the CEO prized one thing: hard work.*

Commas (,)

Commas act as little pauses and help to make sentences easier to read. Here are four of their main uses:

1. To separate (three or more) items in lists.

   ✓ *The planets closest to the Sun are Mercury, Venus, Earth, and Mars.*

   ✓ *Green, red, or gold would work best for the color of the cake.*

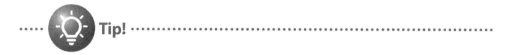

The final comma in a list that comes just before the word "and/or" is known as the "Oxford comma" or "serial comma." Its use is optional and a matter of preference, but it's generally favored in academic writing. Because of this, and because omitting it sometimes muddies the meaning of a sentence, aim to use it throughout your thesis.

If your list includes long descriptions of each item, it can be clearer to separate them with semicolons. For example: "Her shopping list included: three different types of jam, including lingonberry; a new frying pan that could also be used in the oven; and a big bag of porridge, which she was hoping would last a month."

2. To join two complete sentences together, using a connecting word like "and," "yet," "while," or "but."

   ✓ *The toddler enjoyed the snow, while his parents wished it would melt.*

   ✓ *The engine started spluttering, but the car kept going.*

 **Tip!**

Joining two sentences together with a comma, but without a connecting word, is known as a comma splice and is an easy mistake to make. For example, in formal writing these sentences are seen as wrong:

✗ *The chillies are hot, only a few are needed for the curry.*

✗ *The gymnast fell off the beam, her score was very low.*

Connecting words need to be added, or colons or semicolons could be used:

✓ *The chillies are hot, and only a few are needed for the curry.* Or: *The chillies are hot: only a few are needed for the curry.*

✓ *The gymnast fell off the beam, so her score was very low.* Or: *The gymnast fell off the beam; her score was very low.*

3. To separate phrases in a sentence. A pair of commas (called "bracketing commas") is used to identify a phrase that supplies supporting information in a sentence. See "Relative clauses" above for more on this.

   Here are two examples of sentences with bracketing commas:

   ✓ *The dog, which had been sitting at its owner's feet, went running after the ball.*

   ✓ *All employees in the company, including the managers, will receive Christmas bonuses.*

4. To separate an introductory word or phrase from the rest of the sentence. The comma is added after the introductory word or phrase, before the main part of the sentence starts. (The introductory phrase sets the scene or provides supporting information that helps the reader make sense of the main part of the sentence.)

   A comma is usually added after words or phrases (when they start a sentence) such as "However," "For example," "Meanwhile," "Furthermore," "Nevertheless," and "Consequently."

   ✓ *However, the lecturer disagreed with his students' conclusions.*

   ✓ *Subsequently, the experiment was completed on time.*

For longer introductory phrases, adding a comma can help to make the sentence easier to read and understand:

✓ *After she slipped on some ice, she decided to go running only when the weather is good.*

But sometimes (particularly for shorter introductory phrases) adding the comma is a matter of preference. For example:

✓ *On Monday I went for a walk in the woods.* ("On Monday, I went for a walk in the woods" would also be fine but the comma isn't really necessary—the sentence is clear without it.)

Semicolon (;)

A semicolon is most commonly used to join two complete, connected sentences. (This is different to the colon, which can join incomplete sentences together.) Writers use a semicolon when they want to show that two sentences are closely related or linked together in some way.

✓ *Roald Dahl wrote Charlie and the Chocolate Factory in 1964; the novel was first adapted for film in 1971.*

✓ *Alex Honnold is one of the world's best rock climbers; he was the first person to climb El Capitan in Yosemite National Park without any ropes.*

Semicolons can be followed by connecting words if, in formal writing, the connecting words are allowed at the start of a sentence. So words like "but" or "because" can't be used, but words like "however" and "therefore" can (and are usually followed by a comma). For example:

✗ *The pie smelled delicious; but it was too hot to eat.*

✓ *The pie smelled delicious; however, it was too hot to eat.*

Here's an example to show the subtle differences in meaning between a period, semicolon and colon.[3]

✓ *Claire is stressed. Rafael is unhappy.*

The use of the full stop suggests these two situations aren't linked; they just happen to be occurring at the same time.

✓ *Claire is stressed; Rafael is unhappy.*

The use of the semicolon suggests the two situations are related in some way; it implies that the same thing is causing Claire to be stressed and Rafael to be unhappy. (Perhaps they both work for the same company, which has recently announced it's firing half of its staff.)

✓ *Claire is stressed: Rafael is unhappy.*

The use of the colon suggests Claire is stressed because Rafael is unhappy.

••

Hyphens and dashes (- – —)

Hyphens (-) are used in compound words (two or more words linked together to create a new word), such as "far-fetched," "self-esteem," and "hot-dog." If you're not sure whether a word should be hyphenated, it's best to check a dictionary, as preferences change over time (for example, there's been a gradual shift from "web site" to "web-site" to "website," and from "e-mail" to "email").

Hyphens can also be used to show that certain words in a sentence should be read together. For example, compare the following:

- "The first-class presentation" (the really good presentation) versus "The first class presentation" (the first presentation to happen in the class).
- "The women-hating men" (the men who hate women) versus "The women hating men" (the women who hate men).

In informal writing, **dashes** (– —) can be used to separate phrases in a sentence, as a kind of more obtrusive comma. In formal academic writing, dashes should only be used in this way in pairs, to separate out a phrase that interrupts the main flow of the sentence:

✓ *The old panda—who had lived in the zoo for more than 20 years—meditatively munched on the bamboo stalks.* (American English)

✓ *Doe's (1967) research – which received little appreciation from his peers – has recently been rediscovered.* (British English)

As you'll see in these examples, American English tends to use two longer dashes (em dashes) without spaces either side; British English tends to use two shorter dashes (en dashes) with spaces either side.

En dashes (in both American and British English) are also used in ranges:

✓ *In the years 2010–2022*

✓ *Ages 7–15*

Quotation marks

Quotation marks are used to identify speech or quotes (extracts of material taken from elsewhere). In either case, put the quotation marks around the exact words said or written by someone else.

Here's an example. Barack Obama once said: "We need somebody who's got the heart, the empathy, to recognize what it's like to be a young teenage mom."[4] The following use of this quote would be wrong, as the writer has tweaked the start of it slightly so the sentence flows well:

> ✗ *Obama said that a federal judge "needs to be somebody who's got the heart, the empathy, to recognize what it's like to be a young teenage mom."*

Here are two potential ways to fix this (where the words within the quotation marks match exactly what Obama said):

> ✓ *When discussing picking federal judges, Obama said, "We need somebody who's got the heart, the empathy, to recognize what it's like to be a young teenage mom."*

> ✓ *Obama said that a federal judge should be "somebody who's got the heart, the empathy, to recognize what it's like to be a young teenage mom."*

If you're quoting someone who's quoting someone else, use single quotes marks within the double quote marks:

> ✓ *"We need to rethink the 'leveling up' agenda," said Coffey.*

····· **Tip!** ···

British English tends to prefer using single quote marks rather than double quote marks, in general. So with nested quote marks, you would use double quote marks within single quote marks.

···

Block quotes (longer quotations that are separated out from the main text) do not need quotation marks around them. Instead they are usually indented.

Scare quotes are slightly different. This is when quotation marks are put around words or short phrases that the writer wants to distance themselves from—usually because they think the word (or phrase) is odd or inappropriate for some reason, or they want to use it in an ironic or sarcastic way.

✓ *Trump's dismissal of the "fake news" published by newspapers like the* New York Times *has contributed to the rise of the alt-right.* (Here the writer is indicating that they don't really think newspapers like the *New York Times* publish news that is fake or made up.)

Scare quotes can also be used in a more benign way to mean "so to speak"; for unusual or invented words or phrases; or just to set certain words or phrases apart from the rest of the text:

✓ *The "take home" message here is that schools need more money to run properly.*

However you use scare quotes, don't overuse them.

Commonly confused words

Table 16.1 gives some words that are commonly muddled up in academic writing, along with brief definitions and examples.

Words	Meaning	Examples
Accept Except	Accept: to agree, to allow, or to receive something. Except: most often used to introduce an exception (this is true *apart from this*).	*Accept these terms and conditions to join our company.* *She accepted the gift.* *He goes to the gym every day except Tuesdays.* *Except for football, I hate watching sport.*
Advice Advise	Advice: an opinion or recommendation (noun). Advise: to give someone guidance (verb).	*My advice is to order the steak.* *I would advise you to order the steak.*
Affect Effect	Affect: to influence (verb). Effect: an outcome or result (noun).	*Wearing glasses affects how well I can see.* *The effect of wearing glasses is to improve my eyesight.*
Assure Ensure Insure	Assure: to reassure (say that something will be OK). Ensure: to make sure something happens. Insure: to protect with an insurance policy.	*I assure you, the train will arrive on time.* *The driver will ensure that the train arrives on time.* *You can insure your phone for a small extra fee.*

Words	Meaning	Examples
Casual Causal	Casual: relaxed; informal; temporary. Causal: used to indicate a link between two things, to show one causes the other.	*Workers are allowed to dress in a casual way in the office on Fridays.* *There is a causal link between obesity and diabetes.* *Correlation between two variables does not mean there is definitely a causal relationship.*
Complement Compliment	Complement: to go together well. Compliment: to praise someone or something.	*That handbag complements your dress very nicely.* *The lecturer complimented his student's essay writing.*
Continual Continuous	Continual: describes something that happens repeatedly but with breaks in between. Continuous: describes something that happens all the time without interruption.	*Her car keeps breaking down continually.* *The waves pound at the beach continuously.*
Fewer Less	Fewer: use for countable things. Less: use for uncountable things. (In general—there are exceptions.)	*There are fewer than ten tickets left.* *I got fewer than five birthday presents this year.* *My coffee needs less milk.* *They have less money after going on holiday.*
It's Its	It's: short for "it is" or "it has." Its: indicates possession.	*It's horrible weather outside.* *My dog's lost its ball.*
Practice Practise	In British English, "practice" is a noun and "practise" is a verb. (In American English just use "practice" in all situations.)	*She needs to do some piano practice.* *She needs to practise the piano. (British English)* *She needs to practice the piano. (American English)*
Principal Principle	Principal: main or primary (also used for the head of a school or college). Principle: a rule or theory, or an important belief.	*The principal aim of WeightWatchers is to help you lose weight.* *A good financial principle is to save more money than you spend.* *That criminal has no moral principles at all.*

Words	Meaning	Examples
Their There They're	Their: indicates possession. There: indicates place, or is used as part of the phrase "there is"/"there are." They're: short for "they are."	*The children started their game.* *The church is over there.* *There are ten apples.* *They're eating my sandwiches.*
To Too Two	To: indicates direction, or moving toward something (as well as other uses, such as the infinitive form of a verb). Too: as well/in addition, or excessively. Two: the number 2.	*I don't want to go to school tomorrow.* *Where is she moving to?* *I hate mushrooms too.* *There are too many options to choose from.* *Mice have two ears.*
Weather Whether	Weather: the climate/atmosphere. Whether: used to introduce choice or different possibilities.	*The weather tomorrow looks good; it's going to be sunny all day.* *Whether or not you want to pay for it, you have to get driving insurance.*
Were We're Where	Were: past tense of the verb "to be." We're: short for "we are." Where: indicates place.	*We were sad the fair was canceled yesterday.* *We're happy it's snowing today.* *Where is the church?*
Who's Whose	Who's: short for "who is" or "who has." Whose: indicates possession.	*Jenny, who's clumsy, dropped the plate.* *Who's got my hat?* *Whose shoes are these?*
Who Whom	The simplest question to ask here is whether you can replace the word with he/she/they (in which case use "who") or him/her/them (in which case use "whom").	*Who has my handbag?* (He has my handbag) *The seagulls, who ate my ice-cream, flew away.* (They ate my ice-cream) *To whom does this belong?* (It belongs to him)
Your You're	Your: indicates possession. You're: short for "you are."	*Your hair always looks great.* *You're sitting in my chair.*

Table 16.1 Commonly confused words in academic writing

If you've read or skimmed through this whole chapter then you may have found it daunting, but don't feel disheartened: as we said in Chapter 14, it's best to take a pragmatic approach to improving your grammar, punctuation, and spelling. With the limited time you have available, focus on improving the handful of mistakes you make the most often (or the ones that most hinder the clarity of your writing). There are plenty of good, free grammar resources online (and your library and university will certainly have some too), so there is plenty of help available. Use this chapter as a starting point for figuring out what you need to learn more about.

 Thesis writing summary #16

- **Take this whole chapter as a "cheat sheet."** Whenever you're unsure about a grammar, punctuation, or spelling issue, take a quick look at the advice in this chapter and (if it doesn't immediately clear things up) use it as a starting point for investigating the issue in more depth.
- **Include a grammar, punctuation, and spelling round when editing your thesis.** Once you've finished a draft of your thesis, go through it again keeping an eye out for the issues we've discussed in this chapter.

How to edit and finish off your thesis

Let's skip forward now to that point where (after much frustration, perseverance, and coffee) you've managed to type the final word of your thesis and can now call it complete. Take a moment (or perhaps a few days or a week) to rest, recover, and celebrate this huge accomplishment. Then take a deep breath and sit down at your desk again, to edit your thesis, tidy it up, and get everything ready for submission.

Editing your thesis

Editing your own work can be tricky. Even professional editors know the value of getting other people to look over their own writing, because it can be really hard to look at your own work objectively and notice all the little flaws in it. Nevertheless, editing your own work is still very much worth doing. Setting aside the time to carefully read over your whole thesis once or twice can help you to tighten up your writing and correct some of the errors that are all too easy to make and miss when you're in the flow of things. Even little changes, like improving the presentation of your thesis, can make a difference to your final mark.

Some people distinguish between "editing" and "proofreading" when it comes to revising and checking a thesis, where editing happens first and involves rewriting your thesis until you're happy with it. Then proofreading is more of a final check, where you might tweak little things, catch any typos, and tidy up the references, etc. But in a context like finalizing a thesis these tasks are very much located on a continuum with no defined point where editing morphs into proofreading. That's why in this chapter we'll talk about "editing" as an umbrella term to cover revising and checking your thesis.

Here are some tips on how to approach editing your own work:

- **Take a break between writing your thesis and editing it.** If you can, set aside a day or two before you start editing. This allows you to get a bit of distance from the text and consider it more objectively.
- **Try to read your thesis slowly and carefully**, so you see what's really on the page, rather than what you assume is on the page. This is a skill in itself, as it can be very easy to gloss over mistakes as you read. One thing that can really help is to **read out loud**, or **subvocalize** (where you mouth the words silently to yourself as you read, which we came across in a different context in Chapter 4). You could even try **text-to-speech software** that will read your thesis out loud to you. Something else that will help is to print off your whole thesis, if you can, and **read it on paper** rather than on screen.
- **Try to read your thesis critically and objectively.** You want to really engage with what you've written, as you would try to do with any other academic text. Ask yourself if what you're reading really makes sense, and if it's expressed well.
- **Review your thesis a number of times, focusing on something different each time.** This is a trick that professional editors use. Rather than trying to edit your thesis in one go and consider everything at once (which inevitably means that you miss things), take a more focused and methodical approach. Of course, this depends on how much time you've got, but you may find it really helps to edit each chapter at least twice: once to focus on "bigger-picture" concerns (e.g. does the text make sense? Have you included everything you need to?), and once to consider more micro-level stuff (e.g. spelling, punctuation, and formatting). This can even be broken down further, so perhaps on one read through you only focus on checking the references, and on another skim through you only check whether the headings are styled correctly.
- **Be aware of the mistakes you tend to make in your own writing.** In Chapter 14, we talked about the importance of getting personalized feedback on your writing and some ways to gather this. If you can get an idea of the mistakes you're more prone to make when you write, look out for these in particular when you edit.
- **Ask for help.** Consider asking a friend, relative or professional editor or proofreader to take a look at your thesis. Just be aware that there are limitations to what they're allowed to change (your university might have guidelines on this).

- **Use spellcheckers and grammar checkers (with caution).** A spellchecker is definitely your friend, but don't trust it blindly: check each "correction" it wants to make. Grammar checkers also need to be used with caution but can sometimes be helpful in indicating errors.

What to check when editing your thesis

If you have time, we'd suggest breaking the editing process down into two main stages, where you start with the bigger picture and then home in on the details.

The bigger-picture check

The first time you edit your thesis, consider the overall structure and content:

- **Does the thesis include everything it needs to?** Double-check this against your original proposal and/or the plan you used to write your thesis.
- **Is your thesis the right length?** Double-check that your thesis isn't over the word limit (or severely under it).
- **Does the text flow well?** Are paragraphs well-structured? Is information presented in a logical order? Is the overall structure sensible? Is it easy to see how your overarching train of thought develops?
- **Can you cut any irrelevant or repetitive material?** Have you digressed off topic anywhere or included information that doesn't really support your argument? Have you repeated yourself anywhere?
- **Does the text make sense?** Does each sentence make sense to you when you read it back? Can you easily work out what you're trying to say? If not, return to the advice on pages 155–158 on how to simplify your sentences.

Essentially, you want to carefully read through your thesis and check that **it makes sense and it flows well**. You're looking out for anything that seems confusing or muddled. You also want to make sure you've included everything you should.

If you're not sure the structure of a section or chapter works well, one technique you can try is **"reverse outlining."** This is where instead of creating an outline before you write the thesis, you're *extracting* the outline from the thesis itself. Essentially, you want to read each paragraph and summarize it in one sentence. What is the main point that each paragraph is trying to get across? Write that down.

Once you have a list of points, check they make sense when you read them in order. Do they follow a logical chain of thought? Do they flow well? Or are they disjointed and muddled, where it's not really clear how to get from one point to the next? If that's the case, consider whether you need to reorder the points or add in new ones for the overall flow to make sense. Then go back to your thesis and see how you can amend it accordingly.

The micro-level check

Once you're happy with the overall content and structure of your thesis, take a breath and then dive back in to consider your writing at the sentence level. Read through your thesis again and:

- Check that your writing is in a formal, academic style (see Chapter 13).
- Look out for grammar and punctuation mistakes, and misspellings and typos. (See Chapter 16 for more advice on this.) Now would be a good time to run a spellchecker.

You'll also want to check the following, probably one at a time on separate read-throughs:

- **Diagrams:** check that your figures and tables are labeled correctly and presented clearly and consistently. In particular, check the following:
    › Figures and tables are numbered separately and sequentially (e.g. Figure 1, Figure 2, Figure 3 etc. and Table 1, Table 2, Table 3 etc.). If you have lots of figures and tables in your thesis you may want to number them by chapter (e.g. the figures in Chapter 1 are numbered Figure 1.1, Figure 1.2 etc. and the figures in Chapter 2 are numbered Figure 2.1, Figure 2.2 etc.).
    › Each figure and table has a caption (e.g. "Figure 1: Graph to show daily temperatures in July 2023") that accurately summarizes the content of the figure or table.
    › Each figure and table is referenced correctly in the main text (e.g. the main text says "Table 4 shows …" or "This data is presented in Table 4"—and Table 4 is actually the correct table to refer to here, not Table 3 or another table).
    › Figures and tables are presented consistently, e.g. all graphs are drawn in a similar style and all tables look similar.
    › Finally (and most importantly), figures and tables are easy to read and include the information necessary to make sense of them (such as what the X axis on a graph is measuring, or what unit of measurement data is presented in).

- **Citations and references:** check that your citations and references are accurate and correctly styled. In particular, check the following (see also Chapter 15):
    - › Everything taken from elsewhere is referenced (i.e. direct quotes, but also whenever you've talked about other people's research and ideas).
    - › Citations for direct quotes include page numbers.
    - › Citations and references are consistently styled (e.g. if following APA style, then the year of publication is in brackets followed by a full stop, the book title is in italics, the publisher is given, etc.—see also Appendix 1).
    - › Every citation matches up to an entry in your bibliography or list of references.

Formatting and styling

Your university will have guidelines on how to format and style your thesis. The best thing to do is to track these guidelines down and methodically tick off each point. You'll probably need to check the following:

- **The font and font size of the main text.** An easy-to-read font like Helvetica, Arial or Times New Roman in 11pt or 12pt is usually recommended.
- **Headings.** You'll probably have two to four levels of headings in your thesis (such as a chapter title, then a main heading, then a subheading). Is the hierarchy of the headings obvious (e.g. is it easy to tell the difference between a main heading and a subheading)? Are the headings consistently styled (e.g. does every chapter title look the same)? And are the headings nested correctly (e.g. have you used main headings for main topics, and subheadings for subtopics?)
- **Page margins.** How wide should the margins on each page be?
- **Line spacing.** Often 1.5-line spacing or double spacing is recommended for the main text.
- **Paragraphs.** How does the reader know when a new paragraph starts? Is there an extra line of space between paragraphs, or is the first line of each paragraph indented?
- **The alignment of the main text.** For academic writing it's typically left aligned.
- **Block quotes.** How are these differentiated from the main text? Typically they should be indented with single-line spacing.
- **Page numbers.** Where do these sit? Often they should go at the bottom of the page in the center.

- **Footnotes.** How are these formatted? Is there a horizontal line dividing the footnotes from the main text? Do the footnotes use single-line spacing?

Check in particular that style choices are applied consistently throughout your thesis. Tidying up the presentation of your thesis may seem like a waste of time, but a professional-looking thesis will create a good first impression and (more importantly) make your thesis easier to read.

Complete the front matter and extra material

Don't forget the extra material you need to include at the start and end of your thesis. This will vary from university to university and yours should have detailed guidelines on what to include. As above, track these guidelines down and methodically check off each point. You will likely need to include some or all of the following.

At the start of your thesis (also called "front matter"):

- **A title page.** This is a page at the start of your thesis that typically gives the following information: the full title and subtitle of your thesis; your full name; the qualification for which your thesis is being submitted; the name of your university; and the month and year the thesis is being submitted.
- **Abstract.** This is a very brief summary of what your thesis is about (your university may give a word limit, e.g. no more than 300 words).
- **Author's declaration.** This is where you confirm that your thesis is your own original work. Your university may have exact wording you can use.
- **Table of contents.** This is a list of your chapter titles and main headings with page numbers. (Your word-processing program can probably generate this for you, rather than you having to type it out and add in all the page numbers yourself.)
- **List of figures and tables.** This is like your list of contents, but for your figures and tables. List the caption of each figure and the number of the page it appears on, then do the same for your tables.
- **List of accompanying material.** If there's anything you need to submit alongside your thesis (such as audio files or video clips), make a list of this.
- **Acknowledgments (optional).** Here you can thank anyone who contributed to your thesis or supported you in writing it.

At the end of your thesis (also called "back matter"):

- **Reference list and/or bibliography.** The reference list is an alphabetical list of the references cited in your thesis. A bibliography is similar but also contains sources that you consulted during your research but didn't cite in your thesis.

- **Appendices (optional).** Here you can include information that is not essential for understanding the main text and would interrupt the flow of it. Each appendix might include a piece of supporting material such as interview transcripts, the text of a questionnaire, large amounts of research data, or detailed analysis of your research data.
- **Glossary (optional).** This gives definitions of any technical vocabulary in your thesis that readers might not understand the meaning of.
- **Index (optional).** This helps readers to locate information in your thesis by giving the page numbers of where particular terms or phrases are mentioned in it.

Once you've brought all of these bits together and your thesis is completely finalized, check with your university whether you need to print it and submit a physical copy, or whether an electronic copy is fine.

 Thesis writing summary #17

- **Set aside time to edit your thesis.** Editing gives you the chance to check you've included everything important, to tighten up your language and tidy up the presentation, and it will help improve your final mark.
- **Edit your thesis at least twice:** once to focus on the bigger picture (the overall content and structure), and once to consider more micro-level aspects (grammar and punctuation, references, etc.).
- **Format and style your thesis** using your university guidelines.
- **Make sure you've included all extra material** required by your university, such as a title page, table of contents, reference list, etc.

Conclusion: Survived!

Congratulations on getting to this point! Maybe you've already finished your adventure through the great "academic jungle" by successfully completing your thesis or dissertation (in which case, congratulations on this huge accomplishment!). But even if you are still on the journey, you should have at least gained a lot of new knowledge and insights about how to survive and thrive during such a demanding project.

We hope that the new knowledge and skills that you have acquired with this book and throughout your thesis writing journey will also serve you well in future endeavors and challenges. After all, having read this thesis writing survival guide and completed your thesis project, you should now be able to:

- **maintain a positive attitude** and **fight procrastination** during challenging projects,
- use tried-and-tested **project management** tools to plan and implement your future projects,
- quickly **identify and summarize state-of-the art knowledge in any scientific field** you are interested in,
- master **empirical research methods** that you can also apply in a professional context,
- **present data** in a convincing way, and
- confidently **write in a formal yet clear style.**

If you feel that this book has helped you develop these and other "survival" skills during your thesis adventure, or that you got some useful tips and inspiration out of it, it would be great if you could help others in the same situation to find it too. The best way to do this is by leaving a short, honest online review for the book. Other students, and we as authors, will appreciate it!

So here we are at the end of this exciting journey. We're sure it must have been challenging for you at certain points, just as it was for us when we were working on our own thesis projects. But it's exactly these sorts of challenges that help us grow. In this sense, a thesis project is also a journey of personal growth. It's been a great pleasure for us to accompany you as guides on the way, and—as the end of each journey is the start of the next—we wish you all the best for your next learning challenge!

Appendix 1: A super-short summary of APA style guidelines

APA style is one of the most commonly used styles for formatting research papers and citing sources, especially in the social sciences. APA stands for American Psychological Association, and the *APA Style Publication Manual* in its latest edition is the official reference for APA Style.

In this short appendix, we briefly summarize just a few of the most commonly applied APA style rules (there are many more!) from the current (7th) edition of the *APA Style Publication Manual*.

Selected references in APA style

Table A1 provides an overview of how references should appear in the list of references at the end of your thesis.

Type of publication	Example of how to cite it	Further remarks
Journal article	Knoll, C., & Sternad, D. (2021). Identifying global leadership potential. *Journal of Management Development, 40*(4), 253–272. https://doi.org/10.1108/JMD-05-2018-0158	• DOI numbers should be included for articles that have them • *40*(4) means volume 40, issue 4 (issue numbers should always be included) • If you take a journal article from an academic research database, use the same reference as if it were a print journal article
Book	Whittington, R., Rengér, P. Angwin, D., Johnson, G., & Scholes, K. (2020). *Fundamentals of strategy* (5th ed.). Pearson.	• The title of the book is set in italics • Include information about the edition (only) if it's not the first edition • The same format is used for books and ebooks • Publisher location is not included • If the book has a DOI, it is included after the publisher's name

Type of publication	Example of how to cite it	Further remarks
Chapter in an edited book	Sternad, D., & Mödritscher, G. (2021). Qualitative growth: An alternative to solely quantitatively-oriented theories of firm growth. In M. Pirson, D. M. Wasieleski, & E. L. Steckler (Eds.), *Alternative theories of the firm* (pp. 103–119). Routledge. https://doi.org/10.4324/9781003211549	• Cite the individual chapter and its author(s), followed by the title of the whole book and its editor(s) • If the book chapter has a DOI, it is included after the publisher name • For ebooks that have no pages, the page range is not included in the reference
Webpage	World Trade Organization. (2022, July 29). *South Africa initiates WTO dispute complaint challenging EU citrus fruit measures*. https://www.wto.org/english/news_e/news22_e/ds613rfc_29jul22_e.htm	• If there are individual author(s) for an article, use their name(s), otherwise use the name of the organization • Include the date of publication (if available on the website) • Put the title of the webpage in italics
Published doctoral dissertation	Ljungblom, M. (2022). Respect for people: Developing alternative understandings and relationships to ethics, leadership, and culture in lean implementations. [Doctoral dissertation, Uppsala University]. http://uu.diva-portal.org/smash/get/diva2:1652894/FULLTEXT01.pdf	• "Published" for a doctoral dissertation means it is available from a dissertations database (e.g. ProQuest Dissertations and Theses Global), from an archive, or from the website of the university • Include either the URL of the webpage from which you can download the dissertation, or (if not available) the name of the database where it can be found instead
Conference presentation	Sternad, D., & Kennelly. (2022, May 31– June 2). *Everything happens someplace: Place attachment and responsible management behavior* [Conference presentation]. GRONEN Research Conference, Amsterdam, The Netherlands.	• Include the full date of the conference (from–to) • Include both the name and location of the conference

Table A1 APA style citation rules for commonly used publication formats[1]

In-text citations in APA style

In-text citations are made directly in the body of your thesis and include the name of the author(s) and the date of publication.[2] If a source has three or more authors, you just need to include the first author's name followed by "et al." You need to cite both direct quotations and paraphrases. For direct quotations, include page numbers, e.g. "(Sternad & Mödritscher, 2021, p. 104)."

It is possible to use **citations in parentheses** after finishing a sentence or as part of a sentence, e.g. "There are a lot of different definitions of leadership potential (Knoll & Sternad, 2021)." Alternatively, you can use **narrative citations** as part of a sentence, e.g. "Whittington et al. (2020) suggest that …" Table A2 provides an overview of how to deal with different numbers and types of authors.

Number of authors	Citations in parentheses	Narrative citation
1	(Ljungblom, 2022)	Ljungblom (2022)
2	(Sternad & Mödritscher, 2021)	Sternad and Mödritscher (2021)
3 or more	(Whittington et al., 2020)	Whittington et al. (2020)
Institution	(World Trade Organization, 2022)	World Trade Organization (2022)

Table A2 APA citation style for different numbers and types of authors[3]

Secondary citations (where you can't get hold of the original source) should be used sparingly, and are cited like this: "(Bryman, 2008, as cited in Ljungblom, 2022)." In this case, only Ljungblom's work is included in the list of references.

Appendix 2: With the eyes of the assessor

Table A3 can be used as an evaluation guideline for assessing a thesis. You could also use these questions to carry out a self-assessment of your own work before submitting your thesis for grading.

	Assessment*
Introduction	
Does the author provide enough background information to explain the relevance of their study?	
Is the problem statement clearly described?	
Are the research question and the research aim clearly defined?	
Is it clear after reading the *Introduction* how the author plans to answer the research question?	
Can the thesis topic be considered original and innovative?	
Literature Review/Theoretical Background	
Does the *Literature Review* follow a logical structure?	
Are all parts of the *Literature Review* clearly relevant for answering the research question?	
Is the most relevant existing research included in the review (especially recent contributions to the field)?	
Does the author take a critical stance toward the existing literature (e.g. contrasting different views, or identifying strengths and weaknesses of prior research)?	
Does the author develop a conceptual model or hypotheses that explain the phenomena that are supposed to be studied in the thesis?	
Are the conceptual framework or hypotheses supported by convincing arguments based on existing knowledge and theories?	
Method	
Is the chosen method adequate for answering the research question?	
Are the population, the sampling method, and the sample clearly described?	
Is the sample size sufficient?	
Are data collection methods clearly described and applied in a correct way?	
Are data analysis methods clearly described and applied in a correct way?	
Has the author taken adequate steps to ensure research quality (reliability, validity, objectivity)?	

	Assessment*
Results	
Are relevant research results reported in a structured way?	
Are the results clearly linked with the conceptual framework or hypotheses?	
Are visual displays (tables and figures) used in an adequate way?	
Discussion and Conclusion	
Are the research results related to previous research in the *Discussion* part of the thesis?	
Does the author take a critical stance toward their own work (e.g. acknowledging limitations, or considering alternative interpretations)?	
Are the theoretical contributions of the work clearly explained?	
Are implications for practice made evident?	
Is the research question fully answered?	
Formal criteria	
Are an adequate number of sources used?	
Are the sources of appropriate academic quality?	
Are the sources correctly cited (following the institution's citation guidelines)?	
Is complete evidence provided for third-party thoughts (no signs of plagiarism)?	
Is the layout adequate for a thesis (e.g. following style rules for headings, figure and table captions etc.)?	
Is there a traceable audit trail for both data collection and data analysis (e.g. the survey instrument, interview transcripts, and coding tables included in the appendix of the thesis)?	
Writing quality	
Is there a clear structure and flow of the text in all parts of the thesis?	
Does the author develop a strong and conclusive argument?	
Does the author use concise and precise language?	
Is the text free of spelling mistakes and grammatical errors?	

* *Evaluate each point on a scale of 1="criterion not fulfilled" to 5="criterion completely fulfilled."*

Table A3 Possible evaluation criteria for assessing a thesis or dissertation

Appendix 3: Using generative AI tools in your thesis project

Note: *Things are moving extremely fast in the field of generative artificial intelligence (AI), and new tools (or updated versions of existing tools) are released frequently. If developments require it, then we'll post the latest version of this appendix with more up-to-date advice on the companion website of this book at www.econcise.com/ ThesisWriting.*

We are currently experiencing a rapid evolution of **generative AI tools**: computer algorithms that are able to produce text, audio or video content based on "prompts" (the questions you ask or tasks you give the AI tool). The public launch of the AI chatbot **ChatGPT** in November 2022 has sparked a fierce discussion across all higher education institutions about whether and how generative AI tools should be used in academic research.

As a consequence, universities and academic publishers have been developing their own **policies regarding the use of generative AI tools in academic papers**. Some do not allow the use of AI-generated texts in theses and dissertations at all, while others demand that students should disclose whether and in which ways they have applied AI tools. Please make sure to familiarize yourself with the respective rules of your institution before you use ChatGPT or any similar tools.

In addition to potential institutional restrictions, there are also a range of different **reasons why you should be cautious** regarding the use of AI tools:

- Generative AI tools are trained with an incredible amount of data (e.g. Wikipedia articles, other webpages, books, journal articles and so on). As some of the **basic underlying data might be inaccurate or outdated**, so can the resulting texts that the tool produces for you. Thus, beware of the risk of getting "fake facts" from these tools.
- Tools like ChatGPT work with a **predictive language model**. This is an algorithm that makes predictions—based on huge quantities of data—about what the most likely next word is. For example, when a sentence begins with "Thesis writing is" the model predicts the likelihood for continuing the sentence with words like "hard," "fun", or "easy," dependent on the context. Although the likelihood is calculated on large amounts of underlying data, the outcome of this prediction process is not necessarily "correct." Even OpenAI, the company

behind ChatGPT, warns that "ChatGPT sometimes writes plausible-sounding but incorrect or nonsensical answers" and may sometimes "exhibit biased behavior." That's not exactly what you would expect from any thoroughly researched academic work (including your own).

- The tool doesn't tell you which sources it has got its "inspiration" from. Again, this doesn't comply with the basic requirement of an academic paper that you should always **transparently reveal all your sources**.

- ChatGPT is a bit of a grey zone regarding plagiarism (which is taking someone else's ideas directly and claiming that they are your own—but is ChatGPT really "someone else"?). A research team from Penn State University and Mississippi University recently found that it is possible that generative AI systems can "reuse words, sentences, and even core ideas" from existing text, and therefore aren't immune against falling into the **plagiarism trap**, which you will always want to avoid.

Despite all the cautions, there are still potentially useful applications of generative AI models like ChatGPT in a thesis or dissertation project (keeping in mind that you will always need to follow the rules of your university here too):

- The tool could help you to **get inspiration and generate ideas** when you don't know how to proceed, for example regarding finding a suitable research question (with a prompt like *"Develop five possible research questions on how business model innovation is related to internationalization"*), deciding on a thesis title (*"Provide three ideas for a title of a thesis with the following research question: …"*), creating an outline (*"Create an outline for a literature review on the following topic: …"*), or developing arguments (*"What are potential arguments for why X is positively related to Y?"*). This doesn't mean you then have to use what the AI suggested (always remember the limitations described above!), but it might help you get back on track quickly if you run out of ideas.

- You could ask for some **suggestions for literature sources** that you could then use as a starting point for your own further research, for example with a prompt like *"Find 10 sources of academic literature (articles from academic journals published between 2010 and 2020) on effective teamwork in virtual teams."*

- Finally, you might also use an AI tool for **getting feedback** on your line of thinking or writing style, for example with prompts like *"Imagine you are an academic thesis advisor. How would you evaluate the following paragraph in terms of clarity of the argument: …?"* or *"Critically assess the writing style of the following text: … What improvements would you suggest here?"* Again, you probably won't follow all the advice you get from the AI here, but the answers might make you aware of some issues you would then want to work on.

However you would like to use these powerful new generative AI tools, please always keep in mind that the sentences generated by them are obviously not your own, so you can't really claim "authorship" to them. After all, in the end, you will want to be proud of having written **your own thesis or dissertation**—with your name on it, and your own intellectual contribution in it.

Endnotes

Notes for Chapter 1

1 Schwartz (2015), p. 127.
2 Roberts & Hyatt (2019), p. 4.
3 Chang (1998).
4 Roberts & Hyatt (2019), p. 17.
5 Sternad (2021), p. 16.
6 United States Marine Corps (1994), p. 70.
7 Newport (2007), p. 15.
8 Newport (2016).
9 Some of these strategies are also proposed by Adegbuyi (n.d.) and Newport (2016).
10 May & Elder (2018); Uncapher & Wagner (2018).
11 Adegbuyi (n.d.).
12 Newport (2007), p. 16.
13 Clear (2018), p. 164.
14 Branson (2006).
15 Clement Stone (2012).
16 Newport (2007), p. 42.
17 Ibid., p. 46.

Notes for Chapter 2

1 Lamott (1995), p. 19.
2 Parkinson (1955).
3 Roberts & Hyatt (2019), p. 73.
4 Currey (2013).
5 Davis (2017), p. 12.
6 Archer (n.d.).
7 Burkeman (2021), p. 236.

Notes for Chapter 3

1 See also Roberts & Hyatt (2019), pp. 53–54.
2 See also Kornuta & Germaine (2019), pp. 22–24.

Notes for Chapter 4

1 University of York (n.d.).
2 Most of these tips are based on ideas from Booth et al. (2008), pp. 95–100.
3 Booth et al. (2008), p. 97.

Notes for Chapter 5

1 Roberts & Hyatt (2019), p. 101.
2 Kornuta & Germaine (2019), p. 24.
3 Ibid., p. 28.

Notes for Chapter 6

1 Kornuta & Germaine (2019), p. 21.
2 Dale Bloomberg & Volpe (2018).
3 Roberts & Hyatt (2019), p. 113.
4 University of Edinburgh (2021).

5   University of Reading (2019).
6   Roberts & Hyatt (2019), p. 128.
7   Newcastle University (n.d.).
8   Roberts & Hyatt (2019), pp. 126–127.

Notes for Chapter 7

1   Ravitch & Riggan (2017).
2   Merriam & Tisdell (2015), p. 82.
3   Blair (n.d.).
4   Dul & Hak (2008), pp. 67–71.

Notes for Chapter 8

1   Partly inspired by concepts in Wilson et al. (2021).
2   Partly inspired by concepts in umsl.edu (n.d.).
3   Kornuta & Germaine (2019), p. 50.
4   Similar considerations for choosing your research method were proposed by Jansen (2021).
5   See also Jansen (2021).
6   Kornuta & Germaine (2019), p. 53.
7   Gibbert et al. (2008).

Notes for Chapter 9

1   Palinkas et al. (2015), p. 533.
2   Robinson (2014).
3   Moser & Korstjens (2018); Palinkas et al. (2015).
4   Vasileiou et al. (2018), p. 2.
5   Guest et al. (2006), p. 76.
6   DiCicco-Bloom & Crabtree (2006).
7   Some of those tips are based on contents in Harvard FAS (n.d.).
8   Taylor-Powell & Renner (2003).
9   Ibid.
10   Miles et al. (2014), p. 81.
11   Shortened and adapted from Kobin, E. (2021).
12   Miles et al. (2014), p. 91.
13   Ibid. (2014), p. 81.
14   Taylor-Powell & Renner (2003).
15   If you are interested in learning more about this technique, check out www.publichealth.columbia.edu/research/
     population-health-methods/content-analysis or simply use the search term "qualitative content analysis" in a
     web search engine.
16   Anfara Jr et al. (2002); Northcentral University (2022).

Notes for Chapter 10

1   Columbia Center for New Media Teaching and Learning (n.d.).
2   Battaglia (n.d.).
3   At the time of writing, a sample size calculator was available at www.qualtrics.com/blog/calculating-sample-size.
4   Foster & Parker (1995).
5   Robinson (2017).
6   Cohen et al. (1983).
7   Robinson (2017).
8   At the time of writing, Robinson's article was available online in an open access format at https://doi.
     org/10.1002/hrm.21852.
9   The authors would like to thank Professor Anita Kloss-Brandstätter for her kind support in reviewing the contents
     of this table.
10   Duquia et al. (2014); The Writing Center, University of North Carolina at Chapel Hill (n.d.).
11   Field (2017); Field et al. (2012).

Notes for Chapter 11

1 Roberts & Hyatt (2019), p. 169..
2 Ibid., p. 177.
3 Bloomberg & Volpe (2012), p. 11.
4 Bloomberg & Volpe (2012), p. 11; Crossley (2021).

Notes for Chapter 13

1 Oppenheimer (2005).
2 This technique is suggested by Flower (1993).

Note for Chapter 15

1 Brewster (1855).

Notes for Chapter 16

1 Chartered Institute of Editing and Proofreading (n.d.).
2 Dreyer (2020), p. 35.
3 This is inspired by an example in Trask (1997), pp. 45–46.
4 Markon (2009).

Notes for Appendix 1

1 See https://apastyle.apa.org/style-grammar-guidelines/references for more information on using references based on APA style.
2 See https://apastyle.apa.org/style-grammar-guidelines/citations/basic-principles/author-date for more information on in-text citations based on APA style.
3 Ibid.

Notes for Appendix 3

1 OpenAI (2023).
2 Lee et al. (2023).
3 Caulfield, J. & Solis, T. (2023).

List of references

American Psychological Association (2020). *Publication Manual of the American Psychological Association.* 7th ed. Washington, DC: American Psychological Association.

Anfara Jr, V. A., Brown, K. M., & Mangione, T. L. (2002). Qualitative analysis on stage: Making the research process more public. *Educational Researcher, 31*(7), 28–38.

Archer, J. (n.d.). Q&A. https://www.jeffreyarcher.co.uk/qa/. Accessed 8 March 2022.

Battaglia, M. P. (n.d.). Purposive sample. https://methods.sagepub.com/reference/encyclopedia-of-survey-re-search-methods/n419.xml. Accessed 29 July 2022.

Blair, A. (n.d.). *A Language, Not a Letter: Learning Statistics in R.* Chapter 14: Mediation and moderation. https://ademos.people.uic.edu/Chapter14.html. Accessed 1 June 2022.

Bloomberg, L. D., & Volpe, M. (2012). *Completing Your Qualitative Dissertation: A Road Map from Beginning to End*, 2nd ed. Thousand Oaks, CA: Sage.

Booth, W. C., Colomb, G. G., & Williams, J. M. (2008). *The Craft of Research*, 3rd ed. Chicago, IL: The University of Chicago Press.

Brewster, D. (1855). *Memoirs of the Life, Writings, and Discoveries of Sir Isaac Newton*, vol. 1 (Edinburgh: 1855). https://www.newtonproject.ox.ac.uk/view/texts/normalized/OTHE00101. Accessed 8 March 2022.

Burkeman, O. (2021). *Four Thousand Weeks: Time Management for Mortals.* New York, NY: Vintage.

Caulfield, J., & Solis, T. (2023). Using ChatGPT for assignments: Tips and examples. https://www.scribbr.com/ai-tools/chatgpt-assignments/, published 13 February 2023, revised 2 March 2023, accessed 2 April 2023.

Chartered Institute of Editing and Proofreading (2020). Getting to Grips with Grammar and Punctuation UNIT 2: 2.3. Pronouns. *CIEP Getting to Grips with Grammar and Punctuation* course.

Clement Stone, W. (2012). *The Success System That Never Fails.* Hawthorne, CA: BN Publishing.

Clear, J. (2018). *Atomic Habits: An Easy and Proven Way to Build Good Habits and Break Bad Ones.* London: Random House Business Books.

Cohen, S., Kamarck, T., & Mermelstein, R. (1983). A global measure of perceived stress. *Journal of Health and Social Behavior, 24*(4), 385–396.

Columbia Center for New Media Teaching and Learning (n.d.). QMSS e-Lessons: Types of sampling. https://ccnmtl.columbia.edu/projects/qmss/samples_and_sampling/types_of_sampling.html. Accessed 29 July 2022.

Crossley, J. (2021). How to write the conclusion chapter. https://gradcoach.com/dissertation-conclusion-chapter/, published September 2021. Accessed 14 July 2022.

Currey, M. (2013). *Daily Rituals: How Artists Work.* New York, NY: Alfred A. Knopf.

Dale Bloomberg, L., & Volpe, M. (2018). *Completing Your Qualitative Dissertation: A Road Map from Beginning to End.* 4th ed. Thousand Oaks, CA: Sage Publications.

Davis, J. (2017). *Two Awesome Hours: Science-based Strategies to Harness Your Best Time and Get Your Most Important Work Done.* New York, NY: HarperOne.

DiCicco-Bloom, B., & Crabtree, B. F. (2006). The qualitative research interview. *Medical Education, 40*(4), 314–321.

Dreyer, B. (2020). *Dreyer's English: An Utterly Correct Guide to Clarity and Style.* London: Penguin Random House.

Dul, J., & Hak, T. (2008). *Case Study Methodology in Business Research.* London: Routledge.

Duquia, R. P., Bastos, J. L., Bonamigo, R. R., González-Chica, D. A., & Martínez-Mesa, J. (2014). Presenting data in tables and charts. *Anais Brasileiros de Dermatologia, 89*(2), 280–285.

Field, A. (2017). *Discovering Statistics Using IBM SPSS Statistics*. Thousand Oaks, CA: SAGE Publications.

Field, A., Miles, J., and Field, Z. (2012). *Discovering Statistics Using R*. Thousand Oaks, CA: SAGE Publications.

Flower, L. (1993). *Problem-Solving Strategies for Writing*, 4th ed. Boston, MA: Heinle & Heinle.

Foster, J. J., & Parker, I. (1995). *Carrying Out Investigations in Psychology: Methods and Statistics*. Leicester: British Psychological Society Books.

Gibbert, M., Ruigrok, W., & Wicki, B. (2008). What passes as a rigorous case study? *Strategic Management Journal, 29*(13), 1465–1474.

Guest, G., Bunce, A., & Johnson, L. (2006). How many interviews are enough? An experiment with data saturation and variability. *Field Methods, 18*(1), 59–82.

Harvard FAS (n.d.). Some strategies for qualitative interviews. https://sociology.fas.harvard.edu/files/sociology/files/interview_strategies.pdf. Accessed 12 July 2022.

Jansen, D. (2021). How to choose your research methodology. https://gradcoach.com/choose-research-methodology/. Published June 2021, accessed 2 May 2022.

Kobin, E. (2021). From start-up to mature company: Managing organizational crises in high-growth ventures. Master thesis for the International Business Management master's program, Fachhochschule Kärnten/Carinthia University of Applied Sciences.

Kornuta, H. M., & Germaine, R. W. (2019). *The Concise Guide to Writing a Thesis or Dissertation: Educational Research and Beyond*. London: Routledge.

Lamott, A. (1995). *Bird by Bird: Some Instructions on Writing and Life*. New York, NY: Anchor Books.

Lee, J., Le, T., Chen, J & Lee, D. (2023). Do language models plagiarize? *Proceedings of the ACM Web Conference 2023 (WWW '23)*, May 1–5, 2023, Austin, TX, USA. DOI: https://doi.org/\@acmDOI

Markon, J. (2009). Obama's empathy standard drawing heat. http://voices.washingtonpost.com/supremecourt/2009/05/obamas_empathy_standard_drawin.html. Published 21 May 2009, accessed 19 December 2022.

May, K. E., & Elder, A. D. (2018). Efficient, helpful, or distracting? A literature review of media multitasking in relation to academic performance. *International Journal of Educational Technology in Higher Education, 15*(1), 1–17.

Merriam, S. B., & Tisdell, E. J. (2015). *Qualitative Research: A Guide to Design and Implementation*. 4th ed. San Francisco, CA: Jossey-Bass.

Miles, M. B., Huberman, A. M., & Saldaña, J. (2014). *Qualitative Data Analysis: A Methods Sourcebook*, 3rd ed. Thousand Oaks, CA: SAGE.

Moser, A., & Korstjens, I. (2018). Series: Practical guidance to qualitative research. Part 3: Sampling, data collection and analysis. *European Journal of General Practice, 24*(1), 9–18.

Newcastle University (n.d.). Structuring a literature review. https://www.ncl.ac.uk/academic-skills-kit/assessment/dissertations-and-theses/structuring-a-literature-review/. Accessed 12 May 2022.

Newport, C. (2007). *Become a Straight-A Student: The Unconventional Strategies Real College Students Use to Score High While Studying Less*. New York, NY: Three Rivers Press.

Newport, C. (2016). *Deep Work: Rules for Focused Success in a Distracted World*. London: Piatkus.

Northcentral University (2022). Trustworthiness of the data. https://library.ncu.edu/c.php?g=1013606&p=8394398. Published 21 March 2022, accessed 13 July 2022.

OpenAI (2023). Introducing ChatGPT. https://openai.com/blog/chatgpt, accessed 2 April 2023.

Oppenheimer, D. M. (2005). Consequences of erudite vernacular utilized irrespective of necessity: Problems with using long words needlessly. *Applied Cognitive Psychology, 20*(2), pp. 139–156.

Palinkas, L. A., Horwitz, S. M., Green, C. A., Wisdom, J. P., Duan, N., & Hoagwood, K. (2015). Purposeful sampling for qualitative data collection and analysis in mixed method implementation research. *Administration and Policy in Mental Health and Mental Health Services Research, 42*(5), 533–544.

Parkinson, C. N. (1955). Parkinson's law. https://www.economist.com/news/1955/11/19/parkinsons-law. First published in *The Economist* on 19 November 1955, accessed 7 March 2022.

Ravitch, S. M., & Riggan, M. (2017). *Reason & Rigor: How Conceptual Frameworks Guide Research*. 2nd ed. Thousand Oaks, CA: SAGE.

Roberts, C., & Hyatt, L. (2019). *The Dissertation Journey: A Practical and Comprehensive Guide to Planning, Writing, and Defending Your Dissertation*. 3rd ed. Thousand Oaks, CA: SAGE Publications.

Robinson, O. C. (2014). Sampling in interview-based qualitative research: A theoretical and practical guide. *Qualitative Research in Psychology, 11*(1), 25–41.

Robinson, M. A. (2017). Using multi-item psychometric scales for research and practice in human resource management. *Human Resource Management, 57*(3), 739–750.

Schwartz, D. (2015). *The Magic of Thinking Big*. New York, NY: Touchstone.

Sternad, D. (2021). *Solve It! The Mindset and Tools of Smart Problem Solvers*. Moosburg: econcise.

Sternad, D. (2021a). *Developing Coaching Skills: A Concise Introduction*. Moosburg: econcise.

Taylor-Powell, E., & Renner, M. (2003). Analyzing qualitative data. University of Wisconsin-Extension, Program Development & Evaluation paper nr. G3658-12.

The Writing Center, University of North Carolina at Chapel Hill (n.d.). Figures and charts. https://writingcenter.unc.edu/tips-and-tools/figures-and-charts/. Accessed 8 August 2022.

Trask, R. L. (1997). *Penguin Guide to Punctuation*. London: Penguin Reference.

umsl.edu (n.d.). Qualitative research designs. https://www.umsl.edu/~lindquists/qualdsgn.html. Accessed 2 May 2022.

United States Marine Corps (1994). *Warfighting: The U.S. Marine Corps Book of Strategy*. New York, NY: Currency Doubleday.

Uncapher, M. R., & Wagner, A. D. (2018). Minds and brains of media multitaskers: Current findings and future directions. *Proceedings of the National Academy of Sciences, 115*(40), 9889–9896.

University of Edinburgh (2021). Literature review. https://www.ed.ac.uk/institute-academic-development/study-hub/learning-resources/literature-review. Published 10 September 2021, accessed 11 May 2022.

University of York (n.d.). Critical reading. https://subjectguides.york.ac.uk/skills/critical-reading. Accessed 26 April 2022.

Vasileiou, K., Barnett, J., Thorpe, S., & Young, T. (2018). Characterising and justifying sample size sufficiency in interview-based studies: systematic analysis of qualitative health research over a 15-year period. BMC *Medical Research Methodology, 18*(1), 1–18.

Wilson, B., Austria, M.-J., and Casucci, T. (2021). Understanding quantitative and qualitative approaches. https://accelerate.uofuhealth.utah.edu/improvement/understanding-qualitative-and-quantitative-approac. Published 21 March 2021, accessed 2 May 2022.

Index

transferability 108
t-test 120, 134

U

undergraduate studies 2
university library *see library*

V

validity 90, 107, 126–8
variables 47, 61, 71–5
  relationship between them 73, 76, 80, 82
variance (statistics) 119
verb 166, 191
visual displays 133
visual outline 49–50, 53

W

Web of Science 33
Wikipedia 34
wildcards 62
words, commonly confused ones 200–2
work breakdown structure 18–9
workload calculation 19
writing *see also academic writing*
  cautiously 159
  clearly 155
  concisely 157
  critically 172
  descriptive 172
  how to get started 141, 146
  keeping the motivation 149
  like an academic 153
  objectively 161, 162
  precisely 160–1

X

XY scatter plot 125

About the authors

Dr Dietmar Sternad is Professor of International Management at CUAS (Carinthia University of Applied Sciences). He has won several national and international awards for teaching excellence and for the development of outstanding learning materials. His research has been published in leading management journals, including *Entrepreneurship Theory & Practice* and the *Journal of Family Business Strategy*. He is also the author of textbooks (e.g. *Effective Management: Developing Yourself, Others and Organizations*) and international bestsellers (e.g. *Developing Coaching Skills: A Concise Introduction*). Dietmar has many years of experience in supervising thesis projects and enjoys helping students over the many hurdles they face when writing their theses.

Harriet Power is an experienced editor who, after having studied undergraduate and postgraduate degrees at Royal Holloway (University of London), has spent over a decade editing and writing resources for leading educational publishers such as Pearson and Oxford University Press. She specializes in editing books and educational resources that take complex topics and try to explain them in a clear, engaging manner. Harriet is a Professional Member of the Chartered Institute of Editing and Proofreading (CIEP).

Learn key leadership skills, grow as a leader, guide and inspire others!

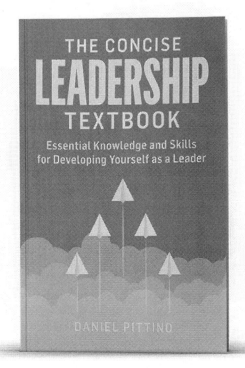

The Concise Leadership Textbook is the ideal companion for students in business and management, as well as in other fields where leadership competences are required, and for professionals who aspire to leadership positions or want to strengthen their leadership abilities.

The Concise Leadership Textbook: Essential Knowledge and Skills for Developing Yourself as a Leader by Prof. Daniel Pittino is available wherever good books and ebooks are sold.

Concise books for smart learners

Apply the strategies and tools of smart problem solving—and succeed in work and life!

What do Albert Einstein, Elon Musk, Sherlock Holmes, and Mahatma Gandhi's six-year old granddaughter have in common? They are all masters of **the art of smart problem solving—** a highly sought-after skill that you can learn, too!

Solve It! The Mindset and Tools of Smart Problem Solvers
by Dietmar Sternad
is available wherever good books and ebooks are sold.

Concise books for smart learners

Made in the USA
Las Vegas, NV
24 February 2024

86162905R00143